W9-CFI-880

The CONNECTED

FAMILY

About the Authors

Claudia Arp and David Arp, MSW, a husband-wife team, are founders and directors of Marriage Alive International, a ground-breaking program providing marriage and family building resources for the church and community. Their Marriage Alive seminar is popular across the United States and in Europe. They are popular speakers, seminar leaders, columnists, and authors of numerous books and video curricula including *Answering the 8 Cries of the Spirited Child,* the 10 Great Dates series, and the Gold Medallion Award–winning *Second Half of Marriage.* Frequent contributors to print and broadcast media, the Arps have appeared on *Today, CBS This Morning,* public television, and *Focus on the Family* radio programs. The Arps have been married for more than forty years and live in Great Falls, Virginia. Web site: www.marriagealive.com.

A smorgasbord of *fun*, *easy*, and PracTICaL
ways to CONNeCT with *your family*

THe CONNEĊTeD

FAMILY

DaviD & ClauDia Arp

HOWARD
PUBLISHING CO.

Our purpose at Howard Publishing is to:
• Increase faith in the hearts of growing Christians
• Inspire holiness in the lives of believers
• Instill hope in the hearts of struggling people everywhere
Because He's coming again!

The Connected Family © 2005 by David and Claudia Arp
All rights reserved. Printed in the United States of America
Published by Howard Publishing Co., Inc.
3117 North 7th Street, West Monroe, Louisiana 71291-2227
www.howardpublishing.com
In association with the literary agency of Alive Communications, Inc.
7680 Goddard Street, Suite 200, Colorado Springs, CO 80920

05 06 07 08 09 10 11 12 13 14   10 9 8 7 6 5 4 3 2 1

Edited by Michele Buckingham
Interior design by Tennille Paden and Stephanie D. Walker
Cover design by Terry Dugan Design

Library of Congress Cataloging-in-Publication Data
Arp, Dave.
    The connected family : a smorgasbord of fun, easy and practical ways to connect with
your family / David & Claudia Arp.
        p. cm.
    ISBN 1-58229-432-1
        1. Family—United States. 2. Interpersonal relations—United States. 3.
Communication—United States. I. Arp, Claudia II. Title.

HQ536.A76 2005
646.7'8—dc22

                                                                    200504369

No part of this publication may be reproduced in any form without the prior written permission of the publisher except in the case of brief quotations within critical articles and reviews.

Unless otherwise indicated, Scripture quotations are from the HOLY BIBLE, NEW INTERNATIONAL VERSION®. Copyright © 1973, 1978, 1984 by International Bible Society. Used by permission of Zondervan. All rights reserved. Scriptures marked NKJV are from The New King James Version, copyright © 1979, 1980, 1982, Thomas Nelson, Inc., Used by permission.

To our incredibly wonderful grandchildren,
Sophie, Hayden, Walker, Benjamin, Lily,
Carson, Azalee, and Jesse

Contents

ACKNOWLEDGMENTS

We are deeply indebted to the many people who contributed to this book and gratefully acknowledge the contributions of the following people:

To those who participated in our parenting groups over the years. Thank you for sharing your helpful family connecting tips.

To those who have pioneered family education and on whose shoulders we stand including Nick Stinnett, John DeFrain, David Olson, Ben Silliman, Dolores Curran, John Gottman, Norm Wright, Emily and Dennis Lowe, Ken Canfield, John Trent, James Dobson, and Gary Smalley. We especially thank Dianne Sollee for all you have done and are doing to encourage marriage and family education.

To our Howard publishing team who have believed and supported this project with great enthusiasm. We especially thank our publisher, John Howard, our editors, Philis Boultinghouse and Michele Buckingham, for their excellent editorial work, and Gary Myers for his great efforts to get the word out about this book.

To Lee Hough and Rick Christian of Alive Communications, for being our advocate and encouraging us along the way.

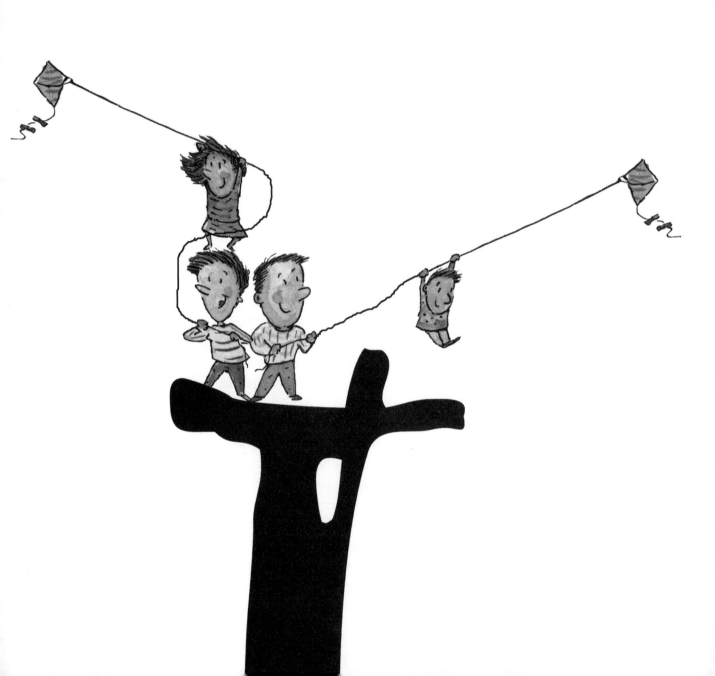

INTRODUCTION

Before You Begin

We were such great parents, *before* we had children! We used to have three parenting theories. Then we had three children, and soon discovered that our theories weren't that helpful. But our hearts' desire was always to have a strong and loving family.

That is probably why you picked up this book. You, like us, want to instill values in your children and have a strong and loving family. But in today's world that is a daunting assignment. It's easy to find information on what not to do—but not so simple to find help for building family strengths.

Scores of books and magazine articles have been written about why families fail.

Certainly, messages from the media and pressure from peers work against building strong families. And as kids grow older, the changing culture makes parenting more difficult.

In the past our culture tended to support family values and served as a safety net, but now our culture is no longer "family friendly." Families face stress on all sides—from inflation, downsizing, and job loss to overscheduled calendars and guilt for not accomplishing more. Children are deprived of things that mean the most—opportunities to enjoy and have fun with their family, time around the dinner table to laugh and talk about the happenings of the day, the in-depth conversations with family members, and the chance to work together to resolve family differences.

Family researcher Dolores Curran observed, "We have focused so long on weaknesses in today's families that we've ignored their strengths."[1] It's no wonder that nearly every family member admits that he or she is looking for some help: help with communicating, help in dealing with conflict, help in strengthening family relationships. Well, we have some good news. That help is here!

In the midst of our stressful world, healthy families do exist! We know so because over the last couple of decades, dedicated family researchers have looked closely at what healthy families do right. For over twenty years, researchers at the University of Nebraska have joined with other universities around the world to study the question, "What constitutes a strong family?"

More than seventeen thousand family members in more than twenty-five countries have been involved in these studies. Prominent researchers like Nick Stinnett, John DeFrain, David Olson, and Ben Silliman have helped to identify the top strengths of strong families.

Based on this body of research, in the following pages we will consider seven characteristics of strong families and will offer you a smorgasbord of fun, easy, and practical ways to strengthen your family in these vital areas. Real ways that real families interact to build family strengths. Take your pick from the many suggested tips and family projects and have fun ensuring that the following seven statements describe your family!

1. Strong families spend time together.

2. Strong families push the positives (or encourage one another).

3. Strong families talk—and listen—to each other.

4. Strong families handle stress and disagreements with grace.

5. Strong families work together and promote responsibility.

6. Strong families promote spirituality and worship God together.

Throughout this book you'll see "Connection sidebars" in gray swatches like this one in the margins. They're filled with fun ideas and suggestions for connecting with your kids or just simple observations about family life. We've left some room for you in some of the margins to write your own "Connection Sidebars." Record your ideas or observations. Make note of something that worked well for your family—or didn't work at all. With your personalized notes, this book could become a family heirloom!

7. Strong families play and have fun together.

WHAT DESCRIBES YOUR FAMILY?

Before we begin, think a moment about how you would describe your family. Perhaps the words "strong and healthy" don't describe your family at all. Maybe your relationships are strained; perhaps your children are constantly arguing with each other and with you. And you may have little hope that things can be different in the future. You may not believe that your family can ever become "strong and healthy."

Let us assure you, tomorrow can be better. You can take steps to build better family relationships. We're not talking about having a perfect family or a family without crisis, stress, or conflict. But we are talking about a resilient family where you love and are committed to each other. Marriage and family counselor Manny Feldman came up with this definition that to us describes the strong family we want to be:

A family is a deeply rooted tree with branches of different strengths, all receiving nourishment from an infinite source.

A family is where character is formed, values are learned, ethics are created, and society is preserved.

A family is where all members contribute and share, cooperate and work, and accept their responsibilities toward the good of the group.

A family is where holidays are celebrated with feasting, birthdays acknowledged with gifts, and thoughts of days gone by kept alive with fond remembrances.

A family is where each can find solace and comfort in grief, pleasures and laughter in joy, and kindness and encouragement in daily living. . . .

A family is a haven of rest, a sanctuary of peace, and most of all, a harbor of love.[2]

To Manny Feldman's definition we'd add that a family is where you can blow it, forget to take out the trash, and still be loved. Brothers and sisters can argue and still be friends. All can be less than perfect and still stick together.

It's great to aim high in our goals as a family, but remember, no one is perfect and no one has a perfect family. You can't have a perfect family, but you can have a strong one! And wherever you are in life, strengthening your family begins with one step. Let us invite you to take it!

Home is the place where we create the future.

—T. Berry Brazelton

Connection One

Spending Time Together

On the way to soccer practice many years ago, our son asked, "Dad, why can't I have my own chauffeur to drive me to soccer practice—or at least my own room, like my friend, Heinrich, does? Whatever Heinrich wants, his dad gives him. Did I tell you how much money he gets for his weekly spending allowance? You won't believe it!"

I (David) listened silently and wondered, *How can I possibly respond to that?* We were living in Vienna, Austria, where Claudia and I worked as marriage and family educators; and while our financial resources were adequate, they were limited. Our three sons attended the United Nations International School, with classmates from many different nations and many different social and economic backgrounds. Most of the families at the school were better off financially than we were. Heinrich's family definitely was. Heinrich's father was a diplomat, and their family lived in a huge house, complete with an elevator. Heinrich not only had his own room; he had his own suite!

There's no way I can compete, I thought. I decided to steer the conversation in a different direction.

"Do you have all your gear ready for the Boy Scout campout this weekend?" I asked. I was going on the campout, too, as an adult leader. I had cleared my work schedule for the whole weekend to make room for the event.

1

Something must have clicked for our son, because he ignored the question and responded, "Dad, Heinrich gets just about everything he wants, but his dad doesn't spend time with him the way you do with me. His dad would never go camping with him. I guess I'd rather be me and have our family the way it is than have lots of stuff and a dad with no time for me."

When you think about it, time is one of the most important things we can give to another human being. Time is a commodity more valuable than wealth. It's a building block for strong family relationships. And it's the starting point for connected families.

If you want to have a strong, connected family, you must spend time together. That's a given. It's the bottom line. But spending time with your family means more than just being together physically. We know families who seem to spend lots of time together, yet we would not describe them as strong, healthy, and connected.

For decades family educators and researchers have debated the merits of "quality time" versus "quantity time." And while it's possible to spend quantity time with your family without having quality time, it's almost impossible to consistently experience quality time with family mem-

bers without finding a reasonable quantity of time to do so.

Of course, family time is not a perfect science. We know families who spend fewer hours together each week on average than other families, yet they demonstrate the traits of strong, connected households. How do they do it? By making sure the limited time they have is invested wisely.

Quality time *and* quantity time are important. Each family must find its own balance, based on its own unique makeup and circumstances.

In this chapter we want to challenge you to use the limited time you have with your family in effective, quality ways that will help you build strong, connected family relationships. We also want to challenge you to spend more actual time with your family members—to find small moments of extra time here and there; to use your time "twice," making it do double duty; and to plan time in your schedule for family togetherness. If you're going to have a connected family, you must spend time together, and the time you spend together must be positive and constructive!

Unfortunately, time is a priceless and increasingly rare commodity in today's world. Maybe your family includes two parents who work outside the home, and the combination of busy work schedules and fatigue makes quality family time hard to come by. Maybe you have one stay-at-home parent, but the demands of housework, community involvement, and children's activities long ago filled in the blanks of an already overcrowded calendar.

Maybe you are parenting alone and must work hard just to make ends meet. You want to have a strong, connected family, yet the task seems more challenging for you than for those parents who are facing it with a partner. Maybe you are a grandparent raising your grandchild, and you don't have the energy you once had to invest in quality family time. Whatever your situation, we want to encourage you and give you suggestions for finding time and investing your time in ways that will lead to a happier, healthier, more connected family.

Tips for Spending Time Together

You can start today finding time for those you love. Don't wait. You will benefit, and so will your whole family. We promise! Don't know where to begin? Here are a few tips:

Tip #1
Stop Saying, "I Don't Have Time"

Our first tip is harder than it sounds: eliminate the phrase "I don't have time" from your vocabulary. The truth is, you *do* have time, if you'll just take it. You may not have as much time as the next person, but almost everyone can find more time for their families if they are willing to look for it.

Does this exchange sound familiar?
Wife: "Honey, can you take a minute and fix this for me?"
Husband: "Sorry, but I don't have the time."

How about this one?
Son or daughter: "Mom, can you give me a little help with my homework?"
Mother: "Not right now. Can't you see I'm busy?"

Here's an action point for you. The next time you're about to say, "I don't have time," substitute the word *love* for *time*. The truth is, love and time go hand in hand. Many times our family members know how much we love them by the time we're willing to spend with them.

Sometimes we're just too inflexible. Yes, there are times when it's legitimate to say, "I can't do that right now." But many times, the problem isn't that we can't; it's that we won't. We have the time; we just choose not to have our own plans interrupted. Those of us who are very structured and goal-oriented by nature must work especially hard to be flexible whenever a family member's request draws on our daily time bank. We need to learn to put down those personal projects and take advantage of family moments when they present themselves. Moments are all we have. How are we using them?

Tip #2
Find Time in the Little Places

It's OK!

Some jobs can wait. If your eight-year-old asks you to play a game with her, put down the mop. You can clean the kitchen floor later. It really is OK to let some things slide!

Sometimes the best way to find more family time is to look in little places. For instance, when you turn off the TV, you find time—time for conversation, interaction, and family togetherness. If the TV seems to monopolize a lot of time in your family, consider putting it somewhere where it's less accessible.

Another place you find family time is around the dinner table. According to developmental psychologists, sitting down to eat together is the most important activity of family life. Researchers have discovered that children who sit down with their families and eat meals together on a regular basis do much better academically, are better communicators, and generally are better adjusted than those children who don't have family mealtimes.

Let us encourage you to make mealtime in your home a family time. Try eating in the dining room or someplace other than the kitchen on occasion. (When the weather is nice, our family loves to eat outside on our porch.) The pots and pans and general kitchen disarray won't distract your attention from your family members.

You can also find family time in the car. Whenever you're driving from place to place with your children, you have a captive audience. So why not fill your car time with conversation, games, and songs? When our boys were growing up, some of the best conversations we had with them took place as we drove them to school and other activities.

Bedtime is another place to find time—time for drawing close, reading stories, talking about hopes and fears, and praying together. Being physically together is best, but it's not absolutely required. One clever dad we know, whose work requires him to travel a great deal, records bedtime stories onto CDs for his three children to listen to when he's away.

They love hearing their dad's recorded messages about his adventures as a little boy. We also know a woman who records herself reading her grandchildren's favorite storybooks, so the kids can listen to the stories in Grandma's own voice as they fall asleep.

Time isn't easy to find. Believe us, we know! But if you look in the little places, you may discover it's already there.

Tip #3
Use Your Time Twice

You can always tell a home with a five-year-old in it: you have to wash the soap before you use it! Perhaps you're in that special stage of family life when you have more dirty soap than time. Finding time for family when life is spelled h-e-c-t-i-c is not always easy. Our recommendation? Look for time you can use twice. For example, when you're folding clothes, let your child put together outfits for kindergarten class. When you're making dinner, recruit your child to help set the table. When you're cleaning up around the house, make a game of picking up toys. Set a timer and tell your child, "See how many toys you can pick up in sixty seconds."

Always look for ways to involve your child in the duties and activities that you have to do anyway. By making the most of the time you spend in life's many small routines, you're sure to add extra family minutes to your day.

Tip #4
Overcome the Overcommitment Disease

What if we told you a disease was killing your entire family? Certainly the shock would cause you to launch a frantic search for the cure! The truth is, there is a disease that is threatening your family life: the disease of overcommitment. If your family is typical, overcommitment has been eating away at your family relationships for years.

We realized life at the Arps was too hectic when the oven broke one Sunday and no one missed it until the next Sunday! Frequently, overcommitment isn't discovered until it's pretty far gone. Here are some symptoms you may be noticing in your own home:

- You've said yes to so many perfectly good activities for yourself and your kids that everyone scatters in different directions each day. Even when you use your oven and cook dinner, no one is home to eat it.

- You've said yes to so many purchases that you have to work extra hours to pay the bills. (Why is it so hard for us to learn that possessions don't build strong families?)

- You've said yes to so many hours of television that you've been robbed of those family multivitamins called "talking together" and "reading together."

- You've said yes to too many hours of surfing the Internet.

Fortunately, while overcommitment has reached epidemic proportions in modern family life, there is a cure. It's free, and it has been around for centuries. No, it's not a capsule you put in your mouth. It's something that comes out of your mouth: the little word *no*. Take a couple of minutes and make a list of commitments and activities you can and should say no to. Try it—it will be good for your family's health!

The truth is, you will never be able to say yes to your family until you learn how to say no to those not-so-necessary activities that rob you of quality family time. Granted, saying no isn't easy. It's especially difficult when you have to say no to perfectly good activities. If saying no is as hard for you as it is for us, then take the following suggestions from Pat King's book, *How to Have All the Time You Need Every Day.* She gives us seven great ways to say no:

1. There's the perfectly valid no: "I've been out three nights this week. I'm staying home tonight and spending time with my family."

2. Then there's the no after you have said yes: "No, I've made a mistake. I shouldn't have committed myself. I'm sorry. I'll have to back out." Then hang up the phone and give a huge sigh of relief.

3. How about the five-star no (this is our favorite: there's no arguing with it): "I'll have to pass it up."

> ### Start Your Own "Morning College"
>
> One smart dad we know created a "morning college." While he shaves each morning, his kids are allowed to ask him any questions they can think of, and he has to do his best to answer.

4. We also like this one. It's the not-right-now no: "I've done it in the past, and I'll do it in the future, but I can't do it right now."

5. For a polite no, say: "I'm sorry, but my schedule doesn't permit me to take on any more obligations this week." You could also use "month" or "year," whichever is appropriate!

6. Along with the polite no is the diplomatic no: "It was so kind of you to think of me. I'm flattered you asked. I'm sorry I won't be able to do it."

7. If all else fails, you can use the absolute no: "I cannot do this. I don't have the desire, the time, the interest, or the energy. No! Absolutely not ever!"[1]

Take it from us: Practice saying no more often, and you'll find that you *do* have the time and energy you need for saying yes to family togetherness.

Tip #5
Take Control of Media, Computers, and Electronic Games

When offered a hypothetical choice of whether to give up TV or give up their father, four-and five-year-olds in a Michigan State University study voted three-to-one to give up Dad! How would your kids vote? What if the choice was between you and the computer, or you and the GameBoy or PlayStation?

Media and electronics are a big part of modern society and a dominant part of many of our children's lives. But throwing out our "competition" may not be the most reasonable solution. A better plan might be to make these things work for us, not against us. How? Here are a few suggestions:

- Let younger children *earn* media time by trading it for an equal amount of time spent reading, doing chores, finishing homework, or practicing skills. Set up a chart to record time spent in each activity.

- Charge a certain amount of money (depending on your child's resources!) for an allotted time of TV viewing or playing computer games. Put the money in a bank and save it for a special family outing.

- Plan ahead. Choose a good family program or video to watch together. Afterward, discuss what you saw.

- When a favorite sport is televised, prepare some snacks, put a blanket on the floor, and have a picnic right in your own home as you cheer together for your team.

Tip #6
Give Focused Attention

One way to assure that we are spending quality time with our family members is to learn how to give focused attention. We all need one-on-one time with those we love. Relationships are always built in twos!

Dr. Ross Campbell, in *How to Really Love Your Child*, defines focused attention this way: "Focused attention is giving a child our full, undivided attention in such a way that he feels without a doubt that he is completely loved. That he is valuable enough in his own right to warrant his parents' undistracted watchfulness, appreciation, and uncompromising regard."[2] Focused attention makes a child feel that he or she is the most important person in the world to Mom and Dad.

How can you give focused attention to your child? For starters, begin a tradition of "just the two of us" times. These are times for you to be alone with just one child, focusing on building that one relationship. We used to make the mistake in our home of doing most things with the entire Arp gang—after all, our children were all boys, and they had similar interests. But somewhere along the line we realized that while group activities are great, you can get to know someone only to a certain point in a group setting.

How well do you know each of your children? What's your child's favorite color? Most loved game? Favorite food? Least favorite subject in school? What is your child's greatest fear? Plan some regular "just the two of us" times, and find out! You may want to schedule these times on a weekly basis. If you have several children, getting together with each one every other week or once a

What Makes a Family Happy?

When fifteen hundred schoolchildren were asked, "What do you think makes a happy family?" few of them replied television, money, fancy homes, cars, or Disney World. Most of the children responded that doing things together and enjoying each other makes a family happy.[3]

Finding One-on-One Time

How can you find that time to give your child focused attention? Look for opportunities like these:

1. *When a younger child is napping, take time with the older one.*

2. *When a brother or sister is at a friend's house, spend time with one child who's at home.*

3. *When an older child is at an activity, do something special with the younger one.*

4. *Go someplace with one child, leaving the others with a baby-sitter.*

5. *Trade off children with friends so that you can spend time alone with just one.*

month might be more realistic. The point is, just do it!

One word of caution: with older kids and teens, you may just have to "wing it." They may not be as open to scheduled "just the two of us" times. Look for those occasional open doors and sporadic communication opportunities. They may seem to always come at the least convenient times, like late at night or when you're tired, but grab the time when it occurs.

Take the opportunity to spend focused time with your children. You'll create a healthier, more connected family, and your kids will be your friends for life!

Projects for Spending Time Together

Project #1
Take a Mystery Minivacation

Here's one way to break the routine in your home! Start by thinking of an unusual place that you've never visited and plan a drive there. Or choose a subject your family might be interested in and turn learning about it into a family field trip. Mystery minivacations don't have to be expensive. Why not set a twenty-dollar limit? It's amazing how much fun can be had on a grand budget of twenty dollars!

Where should you go? What about stables where horses are trained? You could go horseback riding while you're there. Other options might be the newsroom of a local paper or the newborn viewing room of the city hospital. You could visit a fire or observation tower in a forest, climb to the top, and enjoy the view. Or what about a fish hatchery, aquarium, or plant nursery? Our children always loved trips to the zoo—most kids do! If you are really brave, you could visit a pet store; but be sure to take along your will power, or you may come home with a new pet.

As a variation, plan a one-meal vacation. See how many things you can do in your local area over a time period limited to one meal out. Begin right after breakfast, eat lunch out, and be back home in time for a late dinner. Whatever you choose to do, keep your destination a mystery as long as possible to add to the suspense. You're certain to come home with some new memories to add to your family collection.

Project #2
Make an Agenda Box

Make an agenda box together. Get a small shoebox or index-card file box, and let your children enjoy decorating it with markers and stickers. On cards or slips of paper, have family members write down anything they would like the family to talk about during dinner. Take turns drawing from the agenda box when you sit down for a meal, and discuss whatever subjects come up. Be creative and adapt this idea; you might want to make a riddle box or joke box instead.

Project #3
Learn a New Sport

When our boys were young and began to show an interest in sports, we were quick to read the handwriting on the wall. If Dave and I were going to be family participators instead of family spectators, we would have to learn some new skills.

Dave has always been more athletic than I am, but we both agreed to give it a good try. We wanted to choose a sport that we could enjoy together with our children in their adolescent years and into adulthood. Since we lived in Austria, snow skiing was a natural choice—although learning to ski was anything but natural!

We'll never forget those first attempts on the slopes. We all felt quite helpless and inept. Being on the same level—beginners—gave us the feeling of being a team. We were determined to learn, even if it involved pain and suffering.

As you might expect, it didn't take long for our boys to pass us up, but that also worked in our family's favor. The adolescent years are usually a time when children feel that there's little they can do right. Parents always seem to have the edge on experience. But on the ski slopes, the three Arp boys quickly became the experts. They even slowed their pace from time to time to encourage Mom or Dad or give us a short lesson.

Learning to ski together took a lot of time and effort, but we're still enjoying the results.

In fact, as we write this book, we're in the Austrian Alps—our favorite place in the world to write. Just last week our two older sons and four older grandchildren joined us here for a family ski vacation. What a joy it was to see our sons carrying on the tradition of skiing together as a family! And what a challenge it was for us to keep up with them coming down the ski slopes!

If you want to spend time with your children and perhaps interact on a more "even" basis with them, look around and pick a sport you would like to do together. Skiing may not be an option for you. What about tennis, jogging, racquetball, bicycling, or . . . ? You may never make the Olympics, but we guarantee you'll build a stronger, more connected family.

I CAN LIVE for TWO MONTHS
ON ONE GOOD COMPLIMENT.

—Mark Twain

CONNECTION TWO

PUSHING THE POSITIVES

Do you see the glass as half-full or half-empty? In other words, in most things in life, do you tend to focus on the positive or the negative? Your answer has a huge impact on the people closest to you: your family. Strong, connected families push the positives. Instead of dwelling on one another's negative qualities, they support, encourage, and affirm one another.

Megan is one mom who tries to see the glass as half-full. She grew up in a family where academic excellence ruled, so she was somewhat dismayed when her son, Taylor, brought home his first report card with all Cs. *How can someone make all Cs in the first grade?* she wondered. *What will his grades look like in high school? He'll never get into college!* She kept those thoughts to herself, however, and reframed her unspoken first reaction. "Taylor," she said, "this is a fine report card. You're passing everything, but there is plenty of room for improvement. You have great potential!"

In connected families, all things are not positive. After all, no one is perfect, and no family is perfect. But healthy families choose to accentuate the positive. When parents take this approach, children usually follow. Unfortunately, too many of us let our negative thinking lead to self-fulfilling prophecies: "I knew you'd mess up again." "I should have known I couldn't trust you."

"You never tell the truth." What's a kid to do when he or she hears such a stream of negatives? Probably continue with the same negative behavior! Why not, since it's inevitable?

In a University of Nebraska study of three thousand families, researchers found that when parents reframed their thoughts about their children's extreme negative behaviors in more positive terms, they were able to view their children more positively, even when the negative behavior was still present. Reframing helped these moms and dads see the potential in their children's extreme character traits. For instance, the child who is stubborn is also very determined. The messy, into-everything child is very creative and innovative. The child who is bossy could become a great leader someday.[1]

All children—indeed, all people—have a basic human need to feel affirmed and appreciated. Concentrating on the positive is one of the ways we can meet this need in our families. If you're the "half-empty" type and find it easy to see the negative in your children and other family members, we suggest that you refocus on the positive and reserve your negative comments, criticism, and lectures for the family dog!

Tips for Pushing the Positives

How can you begin? Here are five tips to help you start reframing family negatives into positives:

Tip #1
Kick the Discouragement Habit

Before you can push the positives, you have to stop pushing the negatives. You can begin by avoiding negative labels. No one likes being called "slow," "fat," "lazy," or to be known as "the klutz." How discouraging! For the next twenty-four hours, make an effort to listen to yourself when you talk to or about your children. Are you unwittingly labeling them in negative terms? If so, stop!

Another thing to avoid is comparison. Someone once said that comparison is the root of all agony. Comparing one child with another child is definitely harmful, discouraging, and counterproductive. Don't say, "You left a big mess on the table. Why can't you be like your sister? She's so much neater than you are!" Instead, say, "You know, you're very creative. But you need to learn to tidy up after working on a project."

Bottom line: if you want to kick the discouragement habit, you have to practice giving more encouragement. The way to get rid of a bad habit is to replace it with a good one. Try this three-point action plan to help you replace the discouragement habit with the encouragement habit:

Promoting Thoughtfulness

Have you ever noticed that we human beings need absolutely no training in how to be selfish and think only of ourselves? It just comes naturally! Thoughtfulness toward others, on the other hand, requires a more concerted effort—but the results in family connectedness are well worth it.

Here's an idea: why not circulate a "favor key"? A favor key can be any key that you happen to have around the house. Put everyone's name in a hat or bowl and draw out a name. That lucky person gets the favor key first. As the holder of the key, he or she can ask any other family member for a simple and reasonable favor; for example, "Will you let me play with your GameBoy for a few minutes?" Or, "Will you take my turn and walk the dog?" Once that family member does the favor, he or she gets the key and asks a favor of someone else.

The point is to keep the favor key in motion. As it circulates, not only will the key holder have fun, but everyone else will discover how good it feels to do a favor for another person.

- Talk about the pleasant and positive things that are happening in your family. Identify areas in which each of you would welcome one another's encouragement and support.

- Have each family member name one area in particular in which they would like to be encouraged over the next week. Write these down on a card or sheet of paper, and make sure each person gets a copy.

- Now make a commitment to give each other a few encouraging words each day for seven days. If you like how this first week goes, extend the practice for another week.

Remember, encouragement doesn't always have to be verbal. Consider writing encouraging notes as well as speaking encouraging words to your family. Throughout the day, as you think of positive things to tell your spouse and children, write them down in short notes: "I just love the way you smile!" "You looked great in your new jeans today!" "Thanks for cleaning the kitchen." Then leave the notes where your loved ones will find them. Or for an encouraging, nonverbal surprise, buy a bag of balloons, inflate them, and write funny, encouraging, or appreciative messages to a family member on them. Then hang them or place them around the house, or stuff them in closets or drawers that he or she is likely to open.

If you keep this up, before you know it, you will have developed the encouragement habit at your house!

Tip #2
Aggressively Look for the Positive

Would you say the following statement is true or false? "In a healthy family, the positive and good things about family members are obvious and do not need regular attention."

False! False! False! All of us need to be told that we are appreciated—and why we are. Yet many of us tend to notice and bring attention to the negative things about our family members rather than the positive things, to everyone's detriment. Did you know that for every negative statement you speak to a family member, five positive statements are needed to offset its impact? We need to aggressively look for and communicate the positive. Remember, five-to-one is just staying even!

Affirmation is like ammunition: it helps us fight back when circumstances and events outside the home batter our minds and spirits. Why not give your family a shot of affirmation tonight at dinner? (This assumes that you're eating together.) Take turns telling each family member one thing about him or her that you appreciate. We did this exercise with a group of families at a family conference. One mom's comments expressed well the power of affirmation: "It sounded so strange to hear positive words come out of my mouth to describe my teenage daughter . . . but as I said them, they became a reality in our relationship."

Maybe you could proclaim Tuesday night as "appreciation night." Let everyone write appreciative comments about one another on strips of paper. Put the comments in

Promoting Appreciation

Does everyone in your family feel appreciated? If the answer is "no" or "I'm not sure," here are some tips to promote appreciation in your family:

- Make frequent use of expressions, such as "It just wouldn't be the same around here without you."

- Try asking family members for their opinions. We all like to share our thoughts. Dinnertime is a great time to draw one another out.

- Keep memories alive through scrapbooks, home videos, PowerPoint presentations, audio recordings, and pictures. Phrases like, "Do you remember when . . . ?" help create family closeness. One time when our oldest son brought his girlfriend home from college, he and his brothers decided to pull out our family slides. We had fun listening to the boys telling this special gal all about our family history. Apparently it didn't scare her too badly; she and our son are now creating their own family history!

- Don't assume that family members know you love and appreciate them. Tell them—often! Remember, love is the glue that keeps families together.

An Annual Thankfulness Inventory

As you think back over the last twelve months, what are you most thankful for? Too often when we do a self-evaluation, we focus on what we didn't get completed, where we failed, or how tired we are. Unmet expectations are a major cause of disappointment and discouragement. Here's an exercise we do in our family to help us keep the right focus and verbalize all those things for which we are thankful. You may want to do it in your family too.

Give each person a sheet of paper and pencil. Ask everyone to think back over the last year and write down three things they're thankful for. (You do it too.) Was your family in good health? Then write it down! You can get the mental wheels turning by including categories such as:

- *Things I've seen*
- *Things I've learned*
- *Things I've done*
- *Things I've begun*
- *Things I've finished*
- *Things I've decided*
- *Things I've experienced*

Follow up with this question: "What are you looking forward to in the next twelve months?" This thought-provoking exercise is sure to help you develop a more thankful, connected family. Try it!

a box, draw them out, and read them. Next week make it a mystery game: leave off the name of the person who is receiving the compliment and guess who is so fantastic!

Whatever you do, don't be guilty of shooting your own troops with cutting and derogatory remarks! There are enough people out there who will tear us down. In our homes we need to be diligent to look for opportunities to encourage and affirm one another. As one of our sons said, "Home is where you prepare for the battle—not fight it!" Be aggressive in giving your family "affirmation ammunition." This is one battle you can win!

Tip #3
Develop the Habit of Thankfulness

Do you have a thankful family? Given the hurried pace of modern life, most of us need to be reminded to take a few moments to focus on our families and say thank you to God and one another for all the positive things that we see.

You may be thinking, *I should be thankful? For what? You don't know what I'm facing right now!* We do know that life can be difficult at times. Yet through the centuries, people who have been able to look beyond their difficult circumstances and express thanksgiving for the positive things in their lives have fared better emotionally than those people who've surrendered to their negative circumstances.

What is thanksgiving? It's simply giving thanks. To whom? We suggest starting with thanking God for life itself. Then thank him for the many ways you have experienced his blessings in your life and family. Next thank your family members for the support they've given you and for the positive things you see in them. (You'll definitely make them feel appreciated.) Continue by thanking your relatives and friends for the many ways they have encouraged you.

Being thankful has many benefits. Giving thanks creates a healthy attitude in our hearts toward life in general. When we praise and give thanks to God, we are drawn closer to him. And when we thank our family members, we grow stronger, happier, and more connected. It's hard to be thankful and depressed at the same time!

Ultimately, thanksgiving is a daily choice. We can choose to grumble about all the things that are wrong in life, or we can choose to be thankful. Strong, connected families are characterized by gratitude. Is yours?

Tip #4
Share Your Strengths

One way to strengthen your family connection is to share strengths with one another. As we have said, too often we dwell on the negative qualities in each other instead of searching out the positive qualities. To help you concentrate more on the positives, why not share your strengths?

Find a block of time when you can all be together. (That may be the hardest part of this suggestion, but persevere!) Give a card and pencil to those who are old enough to write. For younger members, oral answers will be fine. Have everyone write down one thing that they consider to be a strength in each person in the family. Then take turns sharing your insights with each other. You may be surprised at what you hear! Once when our family was doing this exercise, one of our sons thanked me (Claudia) for being an "emotional pit stop." I had never thought of myself in those terms, but I appreciated the metaphor!

To extend your discussion time, include questions, such as: "What is the greatest strength I bring to our family team?" or, "What is the best thing I like about our family?"

You'll quickly discover that as you affirm your family, you will be affirmed as well.

Projects for Pushing the Positives

Project #1
Start the Red Plate Tradition

One Christmas we received a beautiful red ceramic plate inscribed with the words *You are very special today!* Through the years this plate became one of our most treasured possessions as we used it to celebrate one another on special occasions. Whenever we wanted to make a particular family member feel special, we served his or her meal on the red plate.

Why not start your own "red plate" tradition? One friend of ours loved the idea and discovered a red plate and cup at a pottery factory for one dollar. The plate was christened in their home the day their son had a bike accident and chipped both front teeth. Barely able to eat, he had his dinner on the red plate!

Of course, there's nothing that says your special plate has to be red. It can be whatever color or design you like. You can buy a plate, or you can make one. When should you use the red plate? On birthdays, Mother's Day, Father's Day, when someone wins a school contest, when someone loses a tennis match, when someone studied hard for a test but studied all the wrong things—you get the point! Use it for special days and for days that desperately need to be special.

(You could also try a variation on this theme and start the tradition of the "brave cup." Whenever anyone takes a risk or attempts something new, serve that family member his or her drink in the brave cup that day.)

Project #2
Choose Secret Pals

How would you like to have a secret pal at your house? In our family, having secret pals is one way we've found to build one another's self-esteem and say to each other, "You're special and appreciated." Here's how it works. Write the names of all family members on slips of paper and put them in a hat or bowl. Take turns drawing out names until all the names have been taken. The names you have drawn are your new secret pals!

For the rest of the week, try to do something nice for your secret pal without that person finding out who you are. Some evidences of secret-pal activity in our house have been notes and rhymes left on pillows and on the refrigerator, toys mysteriously picked up, bikes put away, bedsheets turned down and candy left on the pillow, and baskets of clean clothes folded and left in someone's room.

Pals remain secret for one week, and then everyone guesses who his or her secret pal has been. At that point you can redraw names for the next week. Continue drawing new secret pals each week for as long as it's fun for everyone. Try it! In our very me-centered world, it's healthy to encourage one another to do something for someone else.

Project #3
Make a This-Is-Your-Life Notebook

To emphasize how awesome each child in your family is, make a this-is-your-life notebook. Include a section for each year, starting with birth. Include:

- Snapshots

- Artwork

- Favorite sayings

- Names of schoolteachers

- Extracurricular activities

- Accomplishments

- Special celebrations

- Information about friends

- Special outings

- "Firsts"

- Your own commentary

When your children are grown and settled in their own homes, present each with his or her this-is-your-life notebook. They'll be so impressed, they'll probably want to do the same thing for your grandchildren!

Project #4
Plant a Tree

Coordinate your landscaping with special events in your family history. Is an important date coming up on your family calendar? Why not celebrate it by planting a tree? Appropriate events might include:

- Birthdays

- Christmas

- Your child's first day of school

- Losing a tooth

- An accomplishment, such as learning to ride a two-wheel bike

- Any other event you'd like to celebrate and remember

As a family, choose the spot for the memorial tree. Then visit a nursery, select a tree, and plant it together. (If you have access to a wooded area, you could dig up a tree and transplant it to your yard.) Consider adding a marker; on a small piece of treated wood, write what the tree commemorates using a wood burner or indelible ink. It could say something like this: *In honor of Megan's first day of kindergarten, September 5, 2003.*

When our boys were young, they helped plant several trees in our yard. Then we moved and lived outside of the United States for a number of years. When we moved back, it was fun to return to the place of our "roots" and see how much the trees had grown! If you plant memorial trees and then move away, make an effort to go back occasionally to see how your trees have grown. We guarantee you'll feel more connected to your "roots"—and to one another.

A prudent question is one half of wisdom.

—Francis Bacon

CONNECTION THREE

TALKING TO EACH OTHER—AND REALLY LISTENING

From time to time when we lived in Austria, we led our Marriage Alive seminar in our home. Often our kids would sit in the back of the room and listen. One of our sons liked to call himself the "junior-assistant marriage counselor," and he often jokingly offered his assistance to our participants. At times he would repeat back to us some of our own seminar one-liners. "Communication is the breath of life in any marriage," he reminded us one day. Then he added his own twist: "And the Marriage Alive seminar is the mouthwash!"

We laughed, but he was right. One of the most important lifelines in strong marriages and strong, connected families is good communication. Maybe this book is the "mouthwash" that can help you keep your family's communication fresh and positive!

Would you answer the following statement true or false? "Most families have plenty of time to develop good habits and skills in family communication." How we wish that statement were true! Good communication takes time. But in our experience, finding time to really talk and listen to one another is difficult. We had to work hard to find the time to invest in improving our communication with our children as they were growing up. And we still work hard to maintain good communication across the miles and with our grandchildren.

How about you? Is it easy to fall into old habits, get busy, and forget to take the time to really communicate with those you love? Often we say, "Next week won't be so busy. We'll talk then." But next week comes, and we still don't talk together about the issues that are important to us.

Tips for Talking to Each Other— and Really Listening

We want to challenge you: take time *today* to start building a more connected family through better communication. Here are some tips to help you begin:

Tip #1
Choose a Communication Rule of the Week

Psychologists tell us it takes three weeks to make a new habit and six weeks to feel good about it. For the next few weeks, work on creating better communication habits by choosing a "Communication Rule of the Week" and practicing it for seven days. After the seven days, add a new communication rule to your repertoire. For example:

- *Week One:* Stop using "why" questions, which tend to be threatening: "Why do you always leave your room in such a mess?" "Why can't you be neat like your sister?" Better to say something like, "What can we do to make it easy for you to manage your room better?" Ask questions, but phrase them differently.

- *Week Two:* Use "I" statements instead of "you" statements. You'll find you're doing less attacking. It's much better to say, "I get frustrated when the milk is left out on the table" than, "You are so irresponsible when you leave the milk out! Don't you ever think?"

- *Week Three:* Share prayer requests as a family and pray together. For our family, the best time to do this has been over breakfast.

Other communication rules you might adopt include:

- Really concentrate on listening to the answers to your questions.

- Communicate directly with the person involved. Messages sent through third parties can lose clarity or be misunderstood.

- Talk to and about the one you are with.

- Be aware of your nonverbal communication and tone of voice. They are the bulk of your message!

- Don't give unsolicited advice.

- Insert humor into your conversations.

- Look for ways to give compliments.

Remember, good communication is habit forming!

Tip #2
Identify Your Family Communication Center

Have you ever stopped to analyze just where your kids open up and talk the most? In other words, do you know where the communication center is in your house? One thing is for sure: it's *not* where the television is! TV tends to hinder, not help, communication in most families. (We're being repetitive on purpose!)

In our home we tend to have the best family conversations in the living room, especially in the winter when we build a fire. Sometimes we'll slip in there to have a few moments alone to relax, and before we know it, other family members start slipping in too. Great conversations almost always follow.

Maybe the communication center in your home is on the patio or in a bedroom. Maybe it's in the kitchen. Our sons used to come in the kitchen and talk whenever they smelled something good baking in the oven.

For the next couple of days, notice where communication seems to flow most easily at your house. Then hang around that spot, and have your listening ear ready. Leave advice, lectures, and value judgments in the other room, and practice the listening pointers in the next tip.

Tip #3
Be a Good Listener

How do you get a child to talk? Try an art that requires much patience. It's called listening! When parents listen with interest, children feel that their ideas are valued and that they are respected. They develop a sense of self-esteem and confidence as they reason, "Since my parents believe I'm worth listening to, I must be a person of value and importance."

How can you become a better listener?

- *Be attentive.* Stop what you're doing as soon as you can and give your child your full attention. Make eye contact. Be sensitive to nonverbal cues, such as tone of voice and facial expression.

- *Encourage talk.* Smiles, nods, and one-word responses indicate interest. Keep questions brief, open, and friendly, and try to avoid asking "why" questions. Listen; don't react.

- *Empathize.* Try to put yourself in your child's shoes. This may take imagination and patience, but it will help you better understand your child's actions and reactions.

- *Listen with respect.* Try to react to your child as you would to an adult friend. Listen at least as much as you talk. And face the fact that at times kids are complainers; sometimes they just need to get their grievances off their chests.

Learning to listen can help build closeness and connectedness with your children. It can also help them release pent-up emotions and strengthen their ability to make decisions and solve their own problems. Whenever you listen attentively to any person, you pay a high compliment and show that you value what he or she is thinking. So make an effort today. Keep your incoming communication circuits open to those you love.

Three Traits of Good Listeners

1. *Good listeners listen with their eyes. The eye lock is a powerful magnet for making a connection with people. It's a clear sign that you're interested.*

2. *Good listeners give advice sparingly. Nothing cuts off communication quite like giving advice.*

3. *Good listeners never break a confidence. Trust is a tremendous gift. Handle with care by learning to zip your lip.[1]*

Tip #4
Avoid Communication Killers

Do you have communication killers at your house? In a survey conducted at Michigan State University, 79 percent of the parents interviewed said they were communicating with their teenagers. Unfortunately, 81 percent of the teenagers interviewed said their parents were *not* communicating with them! What's wrong with that picture? While younger children may have a better view of their parents' communication efforts, the numbers are telling. Most of us need to work at avoiding those communication killers that prevent open, positive communication with our children, whatever their ages. Here are three to watch out for:

- *Avoid classic put-downs.* When children regularly hear, "You can't do anything right," "You don't know anything about that," or other put-downs, they will withdraw from further conversations.

- *Avoid the higher-volume solution.* When you want to make a point stronger, what do you do? Most of us simply increase our volume. Unfortunately, that causes the other person to counter with even higher volume, which prompts us to get even louder, until both parties end up screaming at each other. The next time you get into a volume contest, try *lowering* your voice. You'll definitely get the other person's attention.

- *Avoid verbal overkill.* Many parents make a statement to their children and then restate their position over and over again. Most children have pretty good hearing, but they can be trained to respond only after hearing something five or six times. A better approach is to make sure your children hear you, state the consequences that will occur if they fail to respond, and then be quiet.

Granted, learning to be quiet is hard work. The tongue is very slippery, and it's easy to let unkind words slide out. Someone once observed, "The difference between a successful family and a mediocre

Two Ears, One Mouth

Did you ever think about the fact that God gave us two ears and only one mouth? Maybe we're supposed to listen twice as much as we are to speak!

one consists of leaving about three or four things a day unsaid!"

Why are we the most unkind to those we love the most? Sometimes we're kinder to strangers than we are to those in our own homes! Would you say the same things and use the same tone of voice with your best friend or boss that you do with your family members? Would you tell a friend that his or her apartment looks like a pigpen or ask, "What's that growing in the kitchen sink?"

One mother said to her four preschoolers when they were arguing, "Children, don't you know the Bible says to be kind to one another?" Her eldest child quickly looked around the room and responded, "It's OK, Mommy. Only family is here." What is it like at your house when "only family" is there? For the next twenty-four hours, listen to the conversations in your home. Pretend you're a guest, and notice what you hear. It may be revealing! Why not start today to treat your guests as family and your family as guests?

Tip #5
Talk without a Hidden Agenda

Once we asked one of our sons, "What tips do you have for parents who really want to communicate with their teens?" His answer

Ten-Minute "Turtle Chats"

Do you have a "turtle" in your house—a family member who lives in the clutter he or she calls a room and only comes out three times a day to eat and grunt at the family? Having meaningful conversations with children or teenagers who live in their shells and only occasionally poke their heads out isn't easy. But you can foster better communication with ten-minute "turtle chats." Try them at bedtime. The silent types will often talk just to delay bedtime a few minutes.

Here are some open-ended statements you can ask your turtle to complete:

- The funniest person I've ever met is . . .
- The strangest place I've fallen asleep is . . .
- A faraway place where I'd like to wake up is . . .
- If I had a million dollars, I'd . . .
- What I can do best is . . .
- My favorite answered prayer is . . .
- My most embarrassing moment was . . .
- What I like about our family is . . .

Granted, tucking your child into bed may take a little longer. But you just may find that your turtle is willing to stick his or her neck out and communicate. See if it works at your house.

was short and to the point. He said, "Talk; don't bug."

Needing a little clarification, we asked him, "What's the difference?"

"Bugging is when you talk in order to get your kid to do something," he said. (We immediately felt guilty!) "Talking is when you communicate and you don't want anything."

Too often, it seems, parents talk to their children with particular goals in mind. Or they talk in order to give advice. Maybe we'd communicate better if we'd save our advice for the family pet! Here's a challenge: for the next twenty-four hours, see how much talking you can do without bugging. This means no advice or subtle manipulation.

We have to tell you, we also asked our son, "What should parents do when they need to get their kids to do something?" His answer? "Bug them!" Maybe if we do a lot of talking, a little bugging is OK!

Projects for Talking to Each Other— and Really Listening

Project #1
Adopt a Family Puppet

If you want to stimulate more communication with your children, consider adopting a family puppet. Puppets are great pets. They don't starve if you forget to feed them, they don't get sick or require shots, and best of all, they don't go to the bathroom on your new carpet!

In Europe we lived in an apartment where we were not allowed to have pets other than hamsters, guinea pigs, or goldfish. So we adopted a puppet named Hans. Hans was a policeman and spoke only German. While Hans helped all of us learn German better, he also helped us with communication in general. As we discovered, puppets are great for younger children who, for whatever reason—embarrassment, shyness, stubbornness, or something else—will not open up. Sometimes kids find it easier to express themselves to a puppet than to an adult.

You can find lots of cute puppets in your local toy store, or you can make your own out of old gloves, socks, or sacks. To get conversations going between your children and their new puppet friend, have the puppet ask open-ended statements, such as:

- If I had three wishes, I'd wish for . . .

- The thing I like most about my family is . . .

- When I grow up, I'd like to . . .

- If I were a parent, I would . . .

- I feel afraid when . . .

- What I like best about myself is . . .

As you and your children share experiences, answer questions, or just talk about what happened during the day with your adopted puppet, you'll be developing good communication skills as well as building memories. Ask Hans—he'll tell you we're right!

Project #2
Play "I Remember"

Sometimes creative ideas originate out of sheer desperation. A number of years ago, I (Claudia) was traveling alone with our three small children. I successfully got the four of us onto our international flight; but when the plane experienced an engine problem, it was turned back to New York in the middle of the night. The next flight didn't leave until late the next afternoon. So, after a tense and sleepless night, the boys and I spent a whole day touring New York City by bus.

When we returned to the airport, we were exhausted. And we still had an hour until boarding time! *How am I going to keep these boys entertained for another hour?* I thought. Feeling desperate, I prayed to God for wisdom and creativity. The result was an idea for a game we call "I Remember."

I asked each boy to think back over the day's bus tour of New York City and try to remember everything he had seen. Then I had the three of them take turns naming what they saw, to find out who could remember the most. Before they had finished, it was time to board the plane! This little game not only helped them remember and catalog the things and places they had seen, it left them with a positive impression of what otherwise could have been remembered as a real disaster day.

In the years since that delayed flight, we have often played "I Remember." It definitely came in handy all those times we were packed in our car like sardines and still had hours to drive. When the kids' grandparents visited us in Austria and we all began to feel sad about their leaving, "I Remember" helped us appreciate the good times we'd had together.

Want to play? Let each person take a turn telling something different that they remember about a particular trip, day, celebration, or event. Keep going as long as anyone can come up with something new. You can play anytime you want to catalog memories:

- In the car on the way home from a family vacation

- At the end of the year, thinking back over all the things that happened in the previous twelve months

- At the end of the summer, thinking back over summer break

- After a visit to the circus, the zoo, or the museum

When a move is coming up, adapt the game and play "I'm Looking Forward To" to prepare your family for the coming transition. However you use our game, we guarantee it will reinforce your memories of those special moments that connect you as a family.

Project #3
Publish a Family Newsletter

You don't have to be a great author or publisher to publish your own family newsletter; you just need a little creativity. A newsletter is a great way to foster good communication with your nuclear family and your extended family. For many years we have published a newsletter for our friends and those involved with us in marriage and family education. Now it's fun to pull out those old letters and reread our family history.

The big decision is whether to publish an e-mail newsletter or the more traditional paper kind. The advantage of an e-mail newsletter is that you don't have to pay postage, and you can electronically add photos, animation, and music. The disadvantage is that not everyone you want to send the letter to is likely to have an e-mail account. And if you're sending it out sporadically—say, once a year—it's likely that many e-mail addresses will have changed between newsletters. These days people seem to change their e-mail accounts fairly frequently in order to take advantage of better rates or different services offered by the various Internet providers.

However you choose to send your newsletter, here are some things to include:

- Recent family accomplishments

- Milestones

- Biggest family goof of the year

- Future plans

- Cartoons and jokes

- Pictures and artwork

If you are sending your newsletter by regular mail, take a clean copy to a print shop and have it duplicated. File one copy away for safekeeping and mail the rest. (Consider using your computer to generate a database and labels for all the recipients.) If you are sending your newsletter electronically, be sure to save a copy on a CD so you'll always have it, even if your computer crashes or you do an upgrade. Why not print a copy of your electronic newsletter for your scrapbook? Even without the animated dancing bears, it will be fun to read in years to come!

When you're wrong, admit it; When you're right, shut-up!

—Ogden Nash

Connection Four

Handling Stress and Disagreements with Grace

Put a bunch of strong-willed Arps together on a ski slope, and besides fun, you're bound to have some stress and a few disagreements.

At one point on a ski trip a few years ago, our five-year-old grandson glared at his dad and said, "You just don't love me, or we would eat lunch somewhere else. They don't have anything I like here. I'm not eating anything, and this just proves that you hate me!"

What had been a very pleasant morning of family skiing turned into a tense time as we waited to see how our son would handle this small crisis. Eating somewhere else was not an option. We were at the very top of the slope, there was only one restaurant, and all of us were hungry and on edge. We watched as our son spoke softly to his son.

"I know you would rather eat at the middle station, but this is where we are eating today," he said. "Let me look in my backpack and see what I can find. Here's a granola bar."

Our grandson, sulking—but avoiding a full-fledged meltdown—slowly gave in to his hunger, took the granola bar, and began eating it. Everyone else ordered lunch. When our food arrived, we noticed that he willingly ate the French fries his dad had ordered for him. It may not have been the most nutritious lunch for a little boy, but diffusing this small crisis was certainly healthy for the rest of the family!

How do you handle small and large crises in your home? The answer to this question is a commentary on how strong and connected your family is. Connected families are able to handle disagreements and crises with grace.

One mother related the following story to us:

On Mother's Day at church, the pastor asked all the mothers to stand. As I stood up, my eight-year-old son tugged at my skirt and said, "Mom, sit down! Only the good mothers are supposed to stand."

I was horrified! Surely the people seated around us heard him. My very spirited son had embarrassed me again, but as I stood there I said to myself, *I'm not going to take his bait! I am not my son!*

How do you respond when your child embarrasses you? What do you do when your daughter says she hates you or your son threatens to go on a hunger strike? Like the mom standing up at church, do you resist taking the bait? Are you able to handle most situations with grace? That's what we want to consider in this chapter.

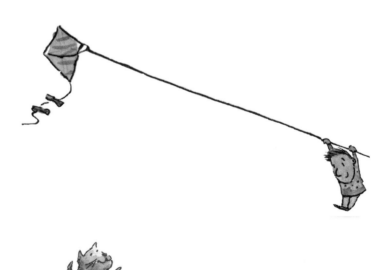

Tips for Handling Stress and Disagreements with Grace

A key to being a strong, connected family is learning how to handle conflict, stress, and crises with wisdom and grace. The following tips can help:

Tip #1
Identify Sources of Family Stress

Some stresses we bring on ourselves. Other stresses come from the high-pressure, fast-paced culture we live in. Is your family suffering from chronic stress? Are you aware of any signs of stress in your children?

Research has determined that one out of every five American high-school students shows some signs of stress. And we have every reason to believe that stress may be prevalent among elementary-school students as well. Kids suffering from chronic stress often exhibit competitiveness and impatience. They tend to internalize anger and seem less confident than other kids. Other symptoms of stress include sweaty palms, rapid heartbeat, muscle tension, and sleeping trouble.

What causes stress in children? A fast-paced, competitive society probably contributes to a large degree. But parents who pressure their children to achieve could also be a cause. We know of one father who, while helping his child complete a research project, gave the poor kid more than one hundred directions in eight minutes!

Stress levels tend to soar at different times of the year. In the fall, children return to school—usually to a new grade, a new class, and a new teacher. That's stressful! At the end

of the school year, another transition takes place. Suddenly their very structured lives are not structured at all. That's stressful too. Then there is the buildup to holidays and the recuperation after holidays. After Christmas can be a particularly stressful time as families deal with the natural letdown and the consequences of possibly having spent too much, eaten too much, and celebrated too much.

Now is a good time to stop and consider these questions:

- Are my children showing symptoms of stress?

- What might I be doing to add to their stress levels?

- What could I do today to relieve stress in my home?

Perhaps this is a stressful time for you and your family. If so, why not do something fun to reduce the stress in your household? Maybe you could surprise your family with their favorite dessert or take your spouse some flowers or share a favorite joke. Be creative and find ways to be a stress reliever, not a stress inducer, in your home.

How To Slow Down Fast-Lane Family Stress

Is your fast-lane life getting out of control? Here are some tips for taking the fast lane a little more slowly:

- *Do the most important things first. Make a list of things you need to do, and then number them according to their importance. If you don't get through your entire list, at least you have done the most important things. At the end of the day, transfer anything undone to a new list for tomorrow, and tear up your old list (go ahead; it will make you feel good).*

- *Group related activities together. If you're out grocery shopping, you might as well stop at the shoe-repair store and the florist on the same trip.*

- *Divide big jobs into workable steps.*

- *Use a timer to see how much you can accomplish in fifteen minutes.*

- *Do all you can to finish a job completely, but don't feel like a failure if you don't get everything done.*

- *Avoid overcommitment by learning when to say no.*

Tip #2
Prepare for and Deal with Crises in a Positive Way

Crises confront every family; and while no one enjoys a crisis, strong, connected

Prescription for Sick Days

Have the sniffles, sneezes, and flu germs invaded your home? If you're a typical family, sometime this year you'll probably answer yes. What can you do when you have a mini-health crisis and a homebound child? Here's our prescription for making the hours and days pass quickly:

- Make your child feel special by keeping a small bell at his or her bedside. Family members can take turns being "on duty" and answering the ring of the bell.

- Make an official medical chart to record diet, medication, temperature, and other important factors that your doctor may need to know. You could also make a countdown calendar to keep track of the days until your patient goes back to school or finishes the antibiotics.

- Turn off the TV and play lots of games. Keep scores and have a family tournament.

- Make a lap desk with an empty cardboard box. Cut a half circle in the two long sides of the box and leave the ends as they are. It will fit nicely over your patient as he or she sits up in bed.

- Cut out comic strips from newspapers and write your own funny lines, or have your child do it.

- Encourage your child to write and illustrate his or her life history.

- For a younger child, make a life-size doll as a bedmate, using old toddler garments for clothing.

Realize that the days you spend at home with a sick child will not be your most productive days. Your to-do list will probably grow longer, not shorter. Relax and grab the opportunity to have that special one-on-one time with your patient. Your love and pampering will be as valuable as any tonic or medication!

families are able to deal with them in a constructive way. If we try, we can always find something positive even in the darkest of situations. Here's how:

- *Before the next crisis, decide now how you will respond.* For example, plan to take a deep breath and count silently to ten before you say anything. Too often we speak before we think and later regret it. If you do overreact, admit it. Once when I (Claudia) realized I was overreacting to a situation, I told my family, "I know I'm overreacting, but somewhere between this reaction and no reaction is the right reaction! Give me a minute and I'll find it."

- *Ask yourself, "What's the worst thing that could happen, and what is good about that?"* Doing this will help you deal with your fears about a particular situation and see things in perspective.

- *Never, never attack family members.* Remember, you are a team, and together you will work things out. Attack the problem, not your family.

- *Look for the humor in the situation.* Learn to laugh together when things get tough.

Crises don't have to be devastating; in fact, they can help strengthen family connections. If handled constructively, tough times can cause family members to pull together rather than be pulled apart as they learn to trust in and rely upon each other.

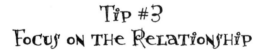

Tip #3
Focus on the Relationship

Someone wisely said, "When it comes to raising kids, rules without relationship lead to rebellion." Often in our desire to be good parents, we concentrate on consistently maintaining the rules in our home, while neglecting to build strong, connected relationships with our children. Focusing on maintaining the rules doesn't make us popular with our offspring. How can we reach a balance in this area—one that is good for our kids and good for family unity and order? Finding this balance was a continual struggle for us during our child-raising years. Here are a few ideas that helped us:

- *Major on the majors, and minor on the minors.* By concentrating on the important things and giving less attention to things that were less important, we found we were able to focus more on our relationship with our children and less on rules. On important things such as moral issues, we remained as steady as the Rock of Gibraltar. On minor things, we tried to be flexible.

- *Recognize that communication is a two-way street.* We tried to really listen to our children, not just talk, correct, and give advice to them. (See previous chapter!)

- *Be willing to say, "I was wrong."* If you're like us, you will find that sometimes your child is right and you are wrong. Don't be too proud to say, "I was wrong; please forgive me."

- *Do things together with your kids.* Plan for those special one-on-one times. Remember, the relationship you build today can be a rebellion preventer later on.

Tip #4
Courageously Guide Your Spirited Child

Is your family blessed with a spirited child—one who exhibits an especially strong will? While some children seem to be born with an easygoing, compliant attitude, others seem to be defiant from the moment they're born. "My daughter gives the term *spirited* a whole new meaning," one parent told us. "It's not that she's inflexible—she's totally brittle." Can you identify?

How To Love a Teenager

Those unique creatures we call "teenagers" are sometimes easy to love. At other times—well, we may need a little help. Here are some ways to get the love flowing:

- *Do things together—biking, backpacking, tennis, Frisbee, shopping, working on the computer, or anything else your teenager likes to do.*

- *Attend important school events, such as athletic games, plays, and open houses.*

- *With enthusiasm, encourage your older teenager to learn how to drive.*

- *Help your teen find an enjoyable job.*

- *Provide transportation with joy and without complaint. Before you know it, your child will have his or her driver's license. Gone will be the great one-on-one times you can have right now driving here and there!*

- *Listen to his or her favorite music—receptively—and discuss it.*

- *Make an honest effort to get to know your teenager's friends. Have an open-home policy. If the gang is ganging up at your house, at least you'll know where your teen is!*

- *Read a book or magazine your teen is reading and talk about it together.*

- *Give generously of your time, presence, and emotional energy. We guarantee it will be one of the best investments you'll ever make!*

Rebuilding Trust

Has your child really blown it? Do you feel you just can't trust him or her anymore? Listen to what Fritz Ridenour says in his book What Teenagers Wish Their Parents Knew About Kids: *"You might as well trust your teenager; you don't have any other reasonable choice. Distrust simply breeds more distrust; but if you keep trusting your teenager, sooner or later the message will get through."*[1] *In other words, even when your child makes a major mistake, you as the parent need to keep trusting that child. You also need to make every effort to avoid speaking or thinking these two trust-busters:*

- *"Earn our trust, and then we'll trust you." How can your child prove that he or she is trustworthy without being given some freedom to make decisions? (Of course, we're not suggesting that when a child blows it in the same area over and over, there shouldn't be consequences.)*

- *"If I can't trust you in this area, how can I trust you in other areas?" Too often when a teenager is irresponsible in one area, the parent generalizes the mistake and applies it to everything else the teen does: "You broke your curfew again, so I can't trust you to be responsible in your schoolwork! You must come directly home after school and study for two hours each day!"*

Trust is not a one-time gift. It must be given again and again.

Understanding that a spirited child is a rather common character—and not necessarily the product of poor parenting—should give some comfort to those parents who face the challenges of shaping a strong-willed son or daughter. The following guidelines can help too. If you have a strong-willed child:

- *Distinguish between willful defiance and childish irresponsibility.* When a child forgets to feed the dog or carelessly loses a sweater, remember that these immature behaviors are typical in childhood. They're not the same as choosing to break a rule or defy a request.

- *Define the boundaries before you enforce them.* Don't assume that your strong-willed child knows the rules. Spell them out before you expect compliance.

- *When your child defiantly challenges you, respond with confident decisiveness.* When you draw a clear line and say, "Don't," and your child looks you in the eye and does it anyway, that's defiance. At times like these, it's important not to give in to your child. Stand firm and apply your predetermined consequence, such as loss of privileges (for example, no television or computer time that day). Your child must know that if he or she defies a rule, consequences will surely follow.

- *After the confrontation is over, reassure your child.* Use this time as a teachable moment. Hold your child close and verbally affirm your love.

- *Avoid impossible demands.* Don't expect your child to be more mature or perfect than you are!

- *Let love be your guide.* Remember, rules without relationship lead to rebellion. But a warm relationship characterized by genuine love and affection is likely to lead to deep family connections, even if you make mistakes as a parent.[2]

Tip #5
Be Willing to Forgive

A memorable line from a '70s-era movie said, "Love means never having to say you're sorry." Except, we would add, about ten times a week when we're wrong, bullheaded, inconsiderate, forgetful, stupid, or lazy! Get the picture?

We have many independent thinkers in our family. When we are all together, it's easy to overreact. We've found that love is being willing to say, "Hey, I blew it again, and I'm sorry!"

Here are a couple of tips for saying you're sorry in the right way:

- *Let your apology reflect back on you.* When you are wrong and have to apologize, avoid attacking the other person. Say, "I'm sorry I overreacted; will you please forgive me?" instead of, "You made me overreact, but I'm sorry anyway."

- *Avoid justifying yourself.* Don't say, "I'm sorry I overreacted, but you would overreact, too, if you were as tired as I am."

Take the initiative in your home. Be the first to say, "I'm sorry." With a little practice, you'll find that it's not too hard at all, and your family will be stronger and more connected for it.

Projects for Handling Stress and Disagreements with Grace

Project #1
Work on Learning How to Handle Anger Appropriately

Have you ever said to yourself, "This is the last time I'm going to get angry"? Doesn't work, does it? Anger is hard to control; too often, it controls us! How can we begin to get a handle on anger and process it appropriately? We suggest working through the following questions first on your own. Later you can work on them as a family project or go through them one-on-one with each family member.

Begin by looking at how you presently deal with anger and how you would like to deal with it in the future. Take some time to reflect on the following questions. You may want to write down your answers:

1. *When do I get angry?* What things and circumstances really anger you?

2. *How do I feel when I'm angry?* Do you feel hurt, frustrated, let down, misunderstood, or violated?

3. *What do I do when I'm angry?* Do you sulk and get silent, or do you throw things, shout, and slam doors?

4. *What do I wish I would do when I'm angry?* Here's a chance to think logically about

what you'd like your response to be when you're upset. Maybe you'd want to express your feelings calmly to the other person involved. Perhaps you'd want to write your feelings in a journal or go for a walk or exercise vigorously.

The next time you're angry, think about your desired response, process that anger, and make your anger work for you. You'll find that anger, when rightly processed, can be constructive in a healthy family.

Project #2
Keep a Meltdown Diary

If you have a very spirited child who frequently melts down, try keeping a "meltdown diary." Note what the circumstances are at the time of meltdown. Did your child miss lunch and was hungry or miss a nap and was tired? Being aware of the circumstances surrounding meltdowns may help you avoid them in the future. For example, the next time you're picking your child up from kindergarten and have to stop off at the market before going home to eat lunch, you'll know to bring along a snack for your child to help extend his or her coping time.

Project #3
Bridge the Generation Gap

Have you ever heard this statement? "But Mom, you grew up in another world!" There's probably some truth there. It is a different world today in many ways. But differences don't have to set off crises. We can bridge the generation gap!

Try this for starters: Challenge your kids to list twenty things that were not yet invented when you were their age. Here are a few things they might come up with:

- Computers
- CDs/DVDs
- Cell phones
- Space shuttles

- PDAs

- Luggage on rollers

- Velcro

- Digital cameras

- Instant messaging

Ask, "Which of these things are the most helpful to you and to society today? Would we be better off without some of them? Why?" To cap off the conversation, pray together and thank God for all the good things you enjoy as a family in today's world. You will not only encourage some interesting communication, you just may see the generation gap get narrower—or even disappear!

Project #4
Make Aggression Cookies

What do you do when things go wrong? Maybe you planned a fun day of outdoor activities but woke up to monsoon rains. Maybe your child came home upset because a bully taunted him at school. Maybe your kids are singing the "We're bored; there's nothing to do" song. All of these are good times to make "aggression cookies"!

This recipe makes fifteen dozen cookies. You might want to cut it in half unless you want to feed an army!

Aggression Cookies

Preheat oven to 350 degrees. Combine:

- 6 cups oatmeal

- 3 cups brown sugar

- 3 cups margarine

- 3 cups flour

- 1 teaspoon baking soda

Mash, knead, and squeeze "until you feel better" and there are no lumps of margarine. Next, form dough into small balls, not quite as big as a walnut, and place on an ungreased cookie sheet. Butter the bottom of a small glass and dip in granulated sugar. Use this to flatten each ball of dough, dipping the glass into the sugar each time you press a cookie. Bake for 10 to 12 minutes. Remove when lightly brown, cool a few minutes, and transfer to a rack to crisp. Store in an airtight container. The dough keeps well in the refrigerator.

Courageous risks are life giving;
they help you grow,
make you brave and better
than you think you are.

—Marie Curie

CoNNECTioN Five

WorKiNG ToGeTHer aND PromoTiNG ResponsiBILiTY

I (Claudia) clearly remember our youngest son's first day in high school.

Before he went out the door, I told him, "I just want to let you know I won't be attending high school with you."

He looked puzzled and must have been wondering, *Has Mom totally lost it?*

I continued: "I've gone to high school three times—once by myself and then vicariously two more times with your brothers. I'm not going to go again with you."

Our son appeared relieved but still confused, so I explained, "For the last six years, I helped your brothers keep up with class assignments and science projects. I'm tired. I'm not going to do it for you. You're on your own."

"Gee thanks, Mom" he replied, still wondering what planet I was from. But in the following weeks, he began to understand what I meant. When he forgot to study for his math test, he asked me why I didn't remind him about it.

My simple answer: "I'm not in high school. You are."

It's not surprising that he quickly developed responsibility for his own schoolwork. And what a relief it was that I didn't have to be responsible!

Children today are crying out for someone to teach them responsibility and self-discipline—two qualities they need, both now and in the future, to be successful in life. But sometimes we parents find it easier to do things for them than to teach them to do things for themselves. Or, because we really want our children to succeed, we simply decide to pitch in to help. That's what motivated me to be the homework monitor for Jonathan's two older brothers. But my overhelping with schoolwork only delayed the boys from assuming responsibility for themselves (which they eventually learned, thankfully!).

Take a trip with us into the future for a moment and picture your family with your children as adults. What kind of relationship would you like to have with each of them? What kind of relationship would you like for them to have with each other? Can you imagine having good times together, talking, laughing, and appreciating one another? Won't it feel good to enjoy your children without feeling responsible for them? But how can you get to that idyllic point?

An old adage says, "If you aim at nothing, you'll probably hit it." As parents we need to foster responsibility and work together with our children to help them grow into mature, responsible adults. Think about what your children need to know about life before leaving home at eighteen or twenty. Will they be ready to function in the adult world? Able to get up on time in the morning? Know how to do the laundry so there is something clean to wear? Manage a checking account? Start a savings plan? Get along with bosses, co-workers, in-laws, and others? Your kids will need to be able to do all these things and more!

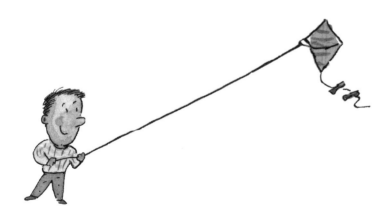

Tips for Working Together and Promoting Responsibility

Ultimately, however, the lesson we need to teach our children is not so much how to do this or that; it's how to be responsible and self-disciplined in all areas of life. Consider the following tips:

Tip #1
Start By Considering Your Own Parenting Style

What's your parenting style? Parents come in all shapes and sizes and with a variety of personalities and parenting styles. Knowing what kind of parent you are is the first step toward effectively helping your children to learn, grow, and mature. See if you can identify your parenting style from the following list:

- *The overachiever parent.* This is the parent who, like a helicopter, hovers over his or her children. It's the mom who weighs the diapers to make sure the baby is getting enough to eat. It's the dad who has shelves loaded with parenting books and videos. I (Claudia) was definitely showing my stripes as an overachiever parent when I gave too much help with our sons' schoolwork. If you're an overachiever parent, step back and make sure you aren't keeping your children from developing responsibility.

- *The hang-loose parent.* If you don't know whether or not this is your parenting style and you really don't care, it probably is! You miss some details, but you get the big picture. Your kids say you're fun to be around—when you are around. But you may not be involved enough in their lives, and you're probably not good at setting consequences and following through on them. (When was the last time you said, "If you haven't cleaned your room by Friday night, you won't be going out with your friends"?) If you're a hang-loose parent, make an effort to be more proactive in setting goals for your children and working together on family projects.

- *The take-charge parent.* This kind of parent is great at setting goals for his or her children—even if the goals are ones the kids could care less about. The take-charge parent likes to give directives; and the more structure, the better. If you have difficulty being flexible and the word *negotiation* isn't in your vocabulary, you're probably a take-charge parent. But if you give all the directives, how can your children ever learn to be self-disciplined? If you're a take-charge parent, try being more flexible and less of a perfectionist. Start working with your children to set realistic goals you all can embrace.

- *The consultant-facilitator parent.* Each parenting style has pluses and minuses, but our favorite style (from the vantage point of having raised three adult sons) is the consultant-facilitator. This is the parent who works with his or her children to help them develop responsibility for their own lives. After all, our children are gifts from God. And our gift back to God as parents is to help facilitate our children's lives—to help them develop responsibility and to guide them to maturity and adulthood.

Tip #2
Remember, You're the Model

Children learn what they live and live what they learn! In other words, if our kids are going to learn how to work together and live responsibly, they're going to learn it from us, their parents. We're the models. For years, as our boys were growing up, we had a poem on our kitchen wall that helped us remember we were modeling for them. Check out the verses and see how you're doing, then strive to model these positive attributes:

If children live with criticism, they learn to condemn.
If children live with hostility, they learn to fight.

If children live with ridicule, they learn to be shy.

If children live with shame, they learn to feel guilty.

If children live with encouragement, they learn confidence.

If children live with tolerance, they learn to be patient.

If children live with praise, they learn to appreciate.

If children live with acceptance, they learn to love.

If children live with approval, they learn to like themselves.

If children live with honesty, they learn truthfulness.

If children live with security, they learn to have faith in themselves and others.

If children live with friendliness, they learn the world is a nice place in which to live.[1]

Stop and think: Have you been modeling criticism or encouragement? Ridicule or praise? Do you live a responsible life? What is the atmosphere like in your home? Remember, children learn what they live!

Tip #3
Help Your Children
Go To Bed at Night

Teaching children to go to bed on their own (or at least to cooperate with the process) is an area of responsibility that many tired parents have told us they'd like help with. Personally, we could always get our kids in bed. The problem was keeping them there! After ten more glasses of water, five trips to the potty, and four more stories, we were usually ready for bed too. We were totally exhausted!

Be a Good Sport

Not all lessons are learned in the classroom. Extracurricular activities, such as sports, help children learn responsibility, discipline, self-control, and respect for authority. They also help kids develop a healthy drive to succeed and teach them how to perform to capacity.

Parents can also be learners. So if you're a soccer mom or a baseball dad, here are some tips for you. Remember, you're modeling!

- Make sure your children know that, win or lose, you love them, appreciate their efforts, and are not disappointed in them.

- Be helpful, but don't coach your children on the way to the game, on the way back home, or at breakfast the next morning.

- Try not to relive your athletic life through your children. This will create pressure you and your kids don't need.

- Avoid yelling at coaches, umpires, referees, and players. This shows bad sportsmanship and embarrasses your children.

How can you take some of the hassle out of bedtime and help children learn (eventually) to put themselves to bed? Here are some of the best tips we've learned ourselves or heard from other parents:

- *Have a bedtime routine.* Children love rituals, so come up with one! Start your new bedtime routine a half hour before you want to turn out the lights and say a final good-night.

- *Give your child a bed buddy.* Children love having a stuffed animal or blanket to cuddle and take to bed with them.

- *Let lights out be lights out.* Once your child is in bed and the lights are turned out, don't read another story, sing another song, apologize, argue, or beg.

- *Never, never entertain or socialize in the middle of the night.* If your child wakes up, be a total bore. Then next morning, you can be your adorable self again.

- *Reward good behavior.* Make a chart and give your child a star for each night he or she goes to bed willingly, stays in bed, and doesn't get up. Give a prize for ten stars.

- *If nothing seems to work, consult your pediatrician.* Your doctor may have some great suggestions for you to try.

- *Don't give up!* Remember that someday your child *will* sleep through the night!

Tip #4
Recruit Some Morning Help

Are mornings nerve-racking in your house? Recruit some help! Mornings are a great time for family members to learn to take responsibility. The fact is, most mornings will go much better if the whole family works together. Here are some tips:

- *Plan ahead.* A few minutes of preparation the night before can make all the differ-

A Bed of Their Own

Whatever we do, however we enforce a bedtime routine, we should never make it rewarding for our children to get out of their beds and come into ours. On those occasions when your kids show up in your room, give them a loving cuddle—then guide them back to their own beds!

ence the next morning. For example, before your children go to bed, have them choose what they will wear to school the next day. Have them organize their school bags and put them by the front door.

- *Share responsibilities.* For example, in our home our sons made their own lunches. Perhaps your children can make their own breakfast or help clean up afterward.

- *Give your children their own alarm clocks.* Make it their responsibility to wake up on time each morning.

- *Create a weekly job chart.* Rotate jobs each week, so no child feels as if he or she is pulling a heavier load.

- *Play happy music.* In the mornings we used to play happy, upbeat music while the boys got ready for school. It helped set a positive tone for the day.

- *Plan one fun family activity for the weekend.* After a structured week, everyone needs a time when they can relax and not watch the clock or feel responsible!

Tip #5
Make Decisions Together

Making decisions together as a family can enrich your sense of family connectedness. It can also teach

Motivating Your Slowpoke To Speed Up

Why is it that when parents are running late, children seem to move at one speed: slow? Kids are experts at stalling, delaying, and dawdling. So how can you speed up your slowpoke? Consider these parent-tested tips:

- *Turn boring routines into a game: "Let's see if you can put four blocks in the basket by the time I count to four."*

- *Establish a routine: "No storytime until your teeth are brushed."*

- *Allow time for your child to transition from one activity to another: "In ten minutes we're going to wash our hands for dinner."*

- *Use an egg timer (a personal favorite of ours): "When the bell goes off, time's up."*

- *Once in a while, say, "Go on and take all the time you need." Then relax and forget the clock!*

- *If nothing seems to work, maybe it's time to adjust your speed and slow down for a while. After all, life's too short to rush through it!*

your children how to make better personal decisions. When a decision needs to be made that affects the entire family, consider the following four-step process:

1. *Define the issue.* What is it that you are trying to decide? Write it down.

2. *Talk about it as a family.* This is the most important part. Be sure to consider both the facts and the feelings about the issue at hand. Research it. Let everyone participate in the process.

3. *Explore possible solutions.* Sometimes the solution is obvious, but most of the time family members will need to compromise their own ideas and each give in a little.

4. *Write down your action points.* Write down what each of you needs to do to carry out the decision you've just made.

5. *Don't procrastinate.* Remember the proverb "Hope deferred makes the heart sick"? Nothing is more discouraging than to make a good decision and never carry it through. Once your family makes a decision, do it!

Projects for Working Together and Promoting Responsibility

Project #1
Overcoming Homework Headaches

Do you have homework headaches? Do your kids forget to do their homework or go off to their rooms and spend more time playing than working? If your children are like most, they want to be near you and all the family action. Doing homework in their own rooms is a real drag.

One clever mom we know came up with a great solution: she created a homework center on the kitchen table. That way, when she was cooking or cleaning or working on family business, she was on call at the homework center to answer questions and to encourage her two children. To keep needed supplies handy, she purchased a cardboard storage box and filled it with supplies. Her children decorated the cardboard with stickers and stencils and christened it the "homework helper box."

Want to make your own homework helper box? Here are some of the supplies you might include:

- Paper

- Pencils

- Pencil sharpener

- Felt-tip pens

- Scissors

- Dictionary

- Glue sticks

- Rulers

To encourage responsibility, we recommend adding a "homework record notebook." Have your children write their assignments in the notebook and check them off when they're complete. When all the homework is done, celebrate with cookies and milk—after all, everyone's already at the kitchen table! You'll be a hero, and homework headaches will be history.

Project #2
Start a Family Business Together

Are you looking for a way to help your children learn more responsibility? Why not start a family business? We remember well the year the Arp boys bought a peanut butter business. We were living in Vienna, Austria, where there was a large international community of peanut butter lovers. But peanut butter—when we could find it—was very expensive. So when one of our boys' friends, who happened to own a peanut butter machine, moved back to the States, he sold them his machine and his list of customers for twenty-five dollars. The Arp Peanut Brothers business was born!

This business venture proved to be an excellent way for the boys to develop a sense of responsibility and see the benefits of hard work. They had to keep financial books and records of time spent, peanuts bought, and jars sold. Each month they received their share of the profits, which was directly related to the amount of time they spent making peanut butter. One month one of the boys earned only fifteen cents, while his brothers earned twelve dollars and five dollars respectively. The next month he got busy and did his share of the work so he could earn a better share of the profits.

The peanut butter business was definitely a family business, because it required our commitment as well. We helped the boys shop for peanuts and drove them around to make deliveries. Sometimes we even helped clean up the mess in the kitchen.

Wasn't it a hassle? Yes! Wasn't it a pain at times? Yes! Was it really worth it? Emphatically, yes! It definitely produced a sense of family connectedness. And years later when one son, at age sixteen, applied for his first official part-time job, he was the only applicant who produced a résumé and the only one who had previously owned a business.

Why not take some family time and brainstorm about a business venture your family could start together? It doesn't have to be something as time-consuming as a peanut butter business. It could be a one-time yard sale to earn money for a special family outing or to help someone you know who has a special need. Whatever you do, you'll find that as you venture out together, you'll help encourage responsibility, create good memories, and build a stronger, more connected family.

Project #3
Choose a Family Service Project

In our fast-paced, self-centered world, it's not always easy to teach children the importance of serving others. But helping our kids experience the joy of doing something for someone else, without any thought of reward or recognition, is a worthy goal. To help accomplish this and build family memories at the same time, we recommend choosing a family service project.

Begin by discussing the idea of a service project with the whole family. There are many things you can do together to serve others. Consider the following suggestions, and choose one that seems best suited to your family's time and resources. Or brainstorm and come up with a project of your own.

- Offer to help an elderly neighbor with some yardwork. You might choose a job that he or she would have great difficulty doing alone.

- Support a child in an orphanage or children's home. You could invite the child to your house from time to time, provide spending money, or give special gifts, such as clothing, books, or toys.

- Check with local authorities and work together to clean up a park area. Be sure to wear protective gloves and warn children about dangerous items and possible biohazards, such as used hypodermic needles or rusty nails.

- Have a family cookie baking night, and send the cookies to a serviceman or college student from the neighborhood. If you don't want to mail the cookies, take them to the local fire station or police station as a gift of appreciation for their service to your family and community.

- Provide transportation to the store, church, or doctor's office for someone in the neighborhood who can't drive or doesn't have a car.

- Volunteer at an animal shelter.

- Here's a good one for computer-smart teens and their parents: teach an older person how to use a computer or the Internet. Volunteer through a senior citizens' center or by posting a notice at a church that is known to have many "senior saints." Prepare to be patient and tactful. You just might end up with an honorary grandparent!

Project #4
Try the Messy-Room Experiment

Are your kids' messy rooms getting you down or making you crazy? Here's an experiment we found helpful to combat the messy-room syndrome. It helped one of our sons turn his room around from disaster area to almost neat. Remembering that it takes three weeks to form a new habit, we challenged our son to keep his room neat and tidy for twenty-one days. To add motivation we offered to give him a dollar a day for each of those twenty-one days.

Certain stipulations applied. For example, no dirty clothes could be stuffed back in drawers, behind the door, or under the bed. Also, the room had to be neat for twenty-one consecutive days. If he missed a day, he had to start counting all over again.

The result? Twenty-one wonderful, nag-free days for us, and some new tendencies toward neatness for Jonathan! We felt successful, he felt successful, and we didn't have to make cleaning his room a major issue. (Postscript: This son is now married and out of our home. His wife is one of the neatest and most organized people we know, and their home is always tidy and clean. Apparently our experiment has had some lasting impact.)

I wonder . . . why at night
When I climb into my bed,
I always feel so extra good
After my prayers are said . . .

—Joan Summer

CONNECTION SIX

PROMOTING SPIRITUAL WELL-BEING

Perhaps you've heard the saying "The family who prays together, stays together." Family researchers Nick Stinnett and John DeFrain would agree with that adage. In their extensive research on families, they discovered that "spiritual wellness" is one of the key characteristics of strong families and that religious involvement as a family unit is a powerful and important source of that strength.[1] Their findings correlate with research by other experts showing a definite correlation between a family's strength and connectedness and the degree of its religious orientation.

In our own work, we have seen that families who embrace the spiritual dimension of life have stronger, more vital connections than families who don't. They tend to have a purpose in life that is bigger than their individual family, and that purpose draws them together. On a personal level, we have found that involving God in our day-to-day family struggles gives us purpose, meaning, and the motivation to relate in a positive way to one another.

What spiritual goals do you have for your family? Do your children know that God is real to you? Do you pray with your children? Are your children aware of answered prayers? The bottom line is: if we want to teach our children to love God, we must love God ourselves and then live out our faith in front of them.

Of course, God has given each of us—including our children—a will to choose him. No guarantees exist that our children will make the wise choice and choose to worship God. But in the Bible we are given a road map to help us live out and share our own faith with our children in a way that will have an impact. In Deuteronomy 6:4–9 we read:

> Hear, O Israel: The LORD our God, the LORD is one. Love the LORD your God with all your heart and with all your soul and with all your strength. These commandments that I give you today are to be upon your hearts. Impress them on your children. Talk about them when you sit at home and when you walk along the road, and when you lie down and when you get up. Tie them as symbols on your hands and bind them on your foreheads. Write them on the doorframes of your houses and on your gates.

A spiritually connected family begins with us. We are to love God with all our heart, soul, and strength. Only then can we influence our children by living out our faith before them, both verbally and visibly: verbally through formal, structured times of teaching and by making the most of informal, teachable moments that arise from time to time; and visibly through modeling a life of faith.

The modeling part is perhaps more challenging. Many parents feel inadequate or imperfect as role models in spiritual matters and, as a result, hold back from sharing their faith with their children. But the truth is, none of us is perfect. And if we want to influence our children and build stronger, more connected families, our faith must be visible.

Tips for Promoting Spiritual Well-Being

Consider the following tips for promoting spiritual well-being in your family:

Tip #1
Plan Family Nights That Promote Fun

"Family night at our home," one mom told us, "is usually a family argument that begins and ends with prayer! It just doesn't work for us."

"We tried it," another parent said. "But it was a real bomb. My twelve-year-old kept rolling her eyes, and our twins had a punching match right in the middle of the Scripture reading. I know family night is something we should do, but how can I get my family to cooperate?"

Hold it right there! Our intention is not to produce guilt or promote family discord. We simply want to add to your family fun and promote spiritual well-being at the same time! Family night (or family day) should be a planned time when you relax with your family and enjoy one another's company. Yes, you may want to include a structured time of family worship that involves singing simple songs together, praying together, or reading a Bible passage or devotional book. But whatever you do, keep the worship time short. Then do something that everyone can enjoy as a group. While family night is an excellent time to work on instilling values and teaching spiritual truths, values and spiritual truths are most often caught, not taught, as your family simply spends time together.

Over the years a high priority in the Arp family has been simply to have fun together!

Family Fun

Are you convinced that family nights are a must for your family? Here are five family-friendly suggestions to get you started:

- Rent a movie together. Pop popcorn, curl up in front of the TV as a group, and then talk about the movie after it's over. Ask, "Who was your favorite character? What positive values did the story teach?"

- Have a game night. Provide special snacks and prizes for everyone. (Ping-pong tournaments were a favorite at our house.)

- Cook a meal together. Homemade pizza is an easy choice: let the little ones play in the dough and choose their own toppings. Follow up with make-your-own-sundaes. Set out several different flavors of ice cream, syrups, nuts, bananas, sprinkles, whipped cream, and cherries, and let everyone go for it!

- Get season tickets to see your favorite sports team. Take the whole family to the home games and cheer on the team together. (Check out local college or semiprofessional teams; tickets are less expensive than for professional games.)

- Produce a family video. If you're really ambitious and technically savvy, add voice-overs and music. Don't forget the ending credits!

Our family nights have produced many great memories, resulting in an ever-deepening sense of spiritual well-being and family connectedness. Want to create your own fun, memory-building family nights? Keep these tips in mind:

- *Don't overstructure your family nights.* Your children are in school for much of the year, and they won't get excited about family night if it feels like school.

- *Plan appropriately.* Know your family's schedules, likes, and dislikes, and plan activities that everyone will enjoy.

- *Be flexible.* You may have planned to play your favorite board game, but everyone else is in the mood to read a book together. Trust the group. Go with the flow!

- *Relax.* Everything doesn't always have to work out just right. Give yourself and your children permission to be less than perfect. Just clean up the messes and move on!

- *Remember why you are doing this.* The purpose of planning family nights is to build deeper relationships and strengthen your family unit. Be sure to include time for talking and joking. And it's OK to be silly!

- *Be aggressive in scheduling family nights.* If you don't make them a priority, they won't "just happen."

Tip #2
Promote Honesty and Openness

Two words that should be in the forefront of every parent's family vocabulary are *honesty* and *openness*. Most healthy, connected families demonstrate a generous dose of both.

What is *openness*? It's being transparent and willing to share those things that are really important to you, such as your faith in God. It's also being open to new experiences. The person who is open hates to get in a rut and is willing to try new things.

Honesty is related to openness; it means telling the truth with love and compassion. You can't fool your children. They know you. So if you want them to grow in their faith, you have to be honest and open with them.

You're going to make mistakes; we all do. Be willing to admit your need for God—even in front of your kids. Especially in front of your kids! Ultimately, being open and honest will help you build your family on a strong spiritual foundation. When *openness* and *honesty* describe the relationships in your home, the whole family benefits. And that's the honest truth!

Try It!

How long has it been since your family did something new or different? Why not try a new activity for family night this week, such as taking a nature hike and thanking God for all you observe? Why not try a new sport, a new restaurant, or a new recipe? Why not have breakfast for dinner? Be open to new experiences and avoid getting into a family rut!

Tip #3
Give Your Family the Gift of Prayer

Prayer is one of the greatest gifts that we parents can give our families. We know our children and grandchildren need our advice; after all, we have lived much longer and have so much good advice to give. But more than our advice, our children need the shield of protection we can provide through prayer!

Don't wait until you're desperate and then resort to "crisis praying." Here are some tips from our friend, Francine Smalley, who is a single mom. Before his death, her husband, Joe, was the director for Athletes in Action for Europe. Left with three small children, Francine knows personally the power of prayer. Here are a few of Francine's tips for praying for your family:

- Pray that God would place a hedge of protection around your children.

- Pray the Scriptures. For example, adapt the words of Jesus in Matthew 6:13 and pray, "Lead _____ not into temptation." When you use the Bible as a prayer guide, you can be assured that you are praying within God's will.

- Pray that your children will have wisdom in selecting friends. We all know how strong peer pressure is today.

- Pray that they would stay pure in this world of relativity, where nothing seems black or white, right or wrong.

- Pray that God will help them make their lives count and use them for his glory.

To Francine's tips we would add two more:

- Pray that God would alert you when your children do something you need to deal with. God answered that prayer for us in interesting ways on more than one occasion. Once at a parents' meeting at our son's middle school, another parent told us our son was known as the "dirty-word dictionary"! That led us to a family study of Proverbs and the power of the tongue.

- Pray for your children's future spouses. We did, and wow, did God answer that prayer in wonderful ways—we now have three fantastic daughters-in-law!

Write It Down

Consider journaling your prayers for your family and loved ones. Then you can rejoice when you see how God answers. Plus, you'll be encouraged to keep praying!

Tip #4
Take Time To Celebrate God's World

Remember: the work will wait while you look at the rainbow, but the rainbow won't wait while you do the work! Recently, after a rain shower, we saw a beautiful rainbow. How relaxing it was to stop, look up, and see the lovely colors spread across the sky!

There are other "rainbows" to enjoy as well—the kind that can be found inside our homes with our families. Maybe you can identify with us. We're both goal-oriented and can get so involved in finishing a task or reaching a goal that it's easy for us to overlook the rainbows along the way. From our work we know that many parents get so involved in providing for and doing things for their children that they miss the simple rainbows:

- Spending a few moments watching a sleeping child
- Taking an extra couple of minutes to sit and laugh together with your kids
- Taking a cookie break (Don't just bake the cookies. Sit down and eat them together!)
- Stopping long enough to watch your children's favorite TV program or to listen to their favorite music CD
- Saying, "Sure, I have time for a game of _____ "
- Touring your yard or a local park and smelling the flowers

Take a few minutes right now. Survey your family and home. You'll be amazed at all the beautiful rainbows you'll find!

Projects for Promoting Spiritual Well-Being

Project #1
Build an Ebenezer To Remember God

In the Old Testament, God's people frequently erected altars or piles of stones at places where they wanted to memorialize something he had done in their lives. In one instance the pile was actually named Ebenezer, from the Hebrew word meaning "stone of help," and subtitled, "Thus far has the Lord helped us" (1 Samuel 7:12).

One family who lived on a farm made a pile of big rocks and painted them with the dates and a short description of the important milestones in their lives: births of their children, the day they laid the foundation of their house, weddings, and so forth. By the time the children were half-grown, it was an impressive pile!

You don't have to live on a farm to have your own Ebenezer though. You can either pick up stones as you find them in your daily life, or buy polished stones from a lapidary, craft store, or landscaping supply company. You can even mix them; use "found" stones to remember a place you visited, a home you had to leave, or a location where you made a life-changing decision. Use the polished ones to mark birthdays, weddings, graduations, and more routine, predictable events. Write the date and event on a piece of cellophane to tape to the polished stones. You can write on regular stones with a pencil. You could even make a simple chart. On the first stone, write "one" and on the chart, for example, "From the forest where we got engaged"; on the next stone, "two," write "From our honeymoon at the beach," and so forth. Keep your stones in a pretty bowl or on a shelf where you can see them and pick them up, with the list, if you made one, nearby.

Your stones don't all have to commemorate happy events, by the way. Sometimes God's love and faithfulness show most vividly through tragedies and difficult times. Perhaps someone in your family forgives a wrong or decides to give up a bitter or angry attitude. Mark it with a stone. Maybe a grandparent has died; pick up a rock from the cemetery. Talk with your family about how "weeping may endure for a night, but joy comes in the morning" (Psalm 30:5 NKJV) and that God's mercies "are new every morning" (Lamentations 3:23). That is the purpose of an Ebenezer: a stone to remind your family of their ever-present Help in trouble.

Project #2
Throw a Birthday Party for Jesus

One Christmas tradition we started when our boys were small was throwing a birthday party for Jesus, complete with coconut cake and candles. (Coconut cake is our family favorite!) I (Dave) grated the fresh coconut, Claudia baked the cake, the whole family sang "Happy Birthday," and the boys blew out the candles.

We always had the birthday celebration on Christmas Eve, preceded by a special meal with our favorite foods. Before serving the cake, we read the Christmas story from the Gospel of Luke and presented our gifts to Jesus. The gifts were not material, but personal—for example, "This year I'm going to work at being kinder to my brothers" or, "I'm going to pray daily for each family member this year." We concluded our birthday celebration by attending a midnight candle-lighting service at our church.

Feel free to adapt this idea for your own family. You could even turn it into an outreach to the children in your neighborhood. Consider hosting a birthday party for Jesus earlier in the month, and include games and simple songs. Ask each child to bring a nonperishable food item, which you will later deliver in Jesus's name to an organization that distributes food to the poor.

Project #3
Create Your Own Nativity Scene

Each Christmas we pull out a very special nativity scene. The little dough figures look the worse for wear. One angel has a broken wing, and her halo is gone. The camel only has three toothpick legs. The wise men have long ago lost their gifts. But the scene still gets center stage at our house. Why? Because it reminds us of one of our most special holiday times.

One Christmas season, when we were living temporarily in the United States, the three boys were bored and restless. All of our Christmas decorations, including our nativity scene, were packed away at our home in Austria. With more time than money or talent, we decided to create our own nativity scene. We made "creative clay" out of ingredients we had on hand in the kitchen and then molded the dough into small figurines. We let the little people and animals dry, then we painted them with tempera paints. The next Saturday we took a walk through the woods and picked up items such as moss, roots, acorns, sticks, stones, and pine cones. We brought our "goodies" home and used them to construct a nativity scene on a piece of plywood. The manger was crafted from a root covered with moss. The pine cones served as trees. The final touch was adding the little people and animals we had made from the dough.

When we returned to our home in Austria, we took our homemade figurines with us. Then each year before Christmas we took a family walk in the woods to pick up new "goodies" to reconstruct the manger scene. How special it has been each year to bring out our little homemade nativity figures—broken wings, broken legs, and all. They bring back great memories of Christmases past!

Want to make your own Christmas figurines? Here's the recipe for creative clay. You only need three ingredients.

Creative Clay

- 1 cup cornstarch
- 2 cups baking soda
- 1¼ cups cold water

Stir the cornstarch and baking soda together. Mix in cold water and stir over medium heat until mixture has the consistency of mashed potatoes. Turn onto a plate and cover with a damp cloth until cool enough to handle. Then knead. Use immediately or store in an airtight container. Your clay figures will dry at room temperature in three days, or you can dry them in a 200-degree oven.

Project #4
Make a Crown of Thorns

Are you looking for a way to celebrate the real meaning of the resurrection of Christ? Consider making a crown of thorns. Here's how:

Use a vine with thorns or a branch from a climbing rose bush or wild blackberry plant. Shape and twist it until it resembles a crown of thorns. As a family, discuss why Jesus was willing to wear a crown of thorns and the significance his sacrifice holds for each of us today.

Next, make a batch of creative clay using the recipe in the previous project, or try this one:

Creative Clay (recipe 2)

- 2 cups flour

- 2 tablespoons salad oil

- 4 teaspoons cream of tartar

Cook over medium heat until a soft, lumpy ball forms (it happens quickly!). Knead for a few minutes until dough is smooth. Store in an airtight container. Dough can be frozen and refrozen several times. If you omit the oil, it will harden and can be painted. Varnish or shellac a finished project to preserve it.

Divide the dough between your family members. Let each person choose either red or blue food coloring and work that color into his or her piece of dough. Store the colored dough in individual airtight plastic bags and leave them by the crown of thorns. Suggest that between that day and Resurrection Sunday, family members make an effort to do kind things for one another. Each time someone does a kind deed for someone else, he or she can take a small amount of dough, form a berry, and cover one of the thorns on the crown. We hope that by Resurrection Day, the crown of thorns will be transformed into a beautiful wreath of berries!

Project #5
Decorate an Easter Egg Tree

Almost everyone has a Christmas tree, but have you ever had an Easter egg tree? This is an Arp tradition we adopted while we lived in Vienna. For the tree, use a branch just as it is, or spray paint it white. You may also use sprigs of pussy willow or forsythia blossoms. Put them in a vase or container, and you have an Easter egg tree all ready for decorating. Here's how to make the decorations:

- Use real eggs. Punch a small hole in both ends of a raw egg. Use an ice pick to break the yolk. Holding the egg over a bowl, blow on one end. With a little effort, the yolk and white of the egg should be forced out of the hole on the other end of the egg and into the bowl. (This may be the evening to have omelets for dinner!)

- Paint the eggs in a variety of colors and place them in an old egg carton to dry.

- Now the fun! Decorate the eggs any way you want to. You can paint designs on them—hearts, flowers, crosses. You can also glue on rickrack, yarn, felt, or other creative materials. (One year one of our boys cut out little pieces of felt and made an empty tomb on his egg.)

- Cut yarn into eight-inch lengths. Thread the yarn through the two holes in each egg. Tie a large knot in the end so the yarn will stay and not pull through. Use the other end of the yarn to tie the egg onto the tree.

Enjoy your Easter egg tree with your family. Talk about the real meaning of the Resurrection and how God gives new life. Save the egg carton to store your creations until next year. Each year as you pull out your tree, you'll pull out special memories!

If a man insisted always on being serious, and never allowed himself a bit of fun and relaxation, he would go mad or become unstable without knowing it.

—Herodotus

CONNECTION SEVEN

Playing and Having Fun Together

"What you did was really dangerous," one of our sons told us when he was in college.

"What do you mean?" we asked.

"Raising us in a foreign country," he responded, "away from our own extended family, friends, and culture."

We had to admit that some American families we'd known in Vienna had experienced problems with their teenagers. We'd also seen several marriages in crisis. Perhaps our son was correct: maybe living overseas had been a risky move. But we had survived—even thrived.

"What made the difference for our family?" we asked our son. "We all still like each other, and we are all relatively sane."

"You made it fun," he replied. "You made the adventure of living in Germany and Austria fun for us."

We have thought often about what our son said. We believe his comments were quite insightful. In fact, we have come to the conclusion through our work and personal experience that wherever you live, whatever culture you are in, having fun in your family is serious business. Family fun is a problem preventer. Strong, connected families invariably like each other and have fun together.

Tips for Playing and Having Fun Together

How much fun does *your* family have? If you want to strengthen your connections and add more fun to your family life, here are a few tips:

Tip #1
Add Some Humor in Your Home

Is your home a fun place to be? Too often our homes are places of tension and stress. As one successful businessman told us, "I can be lighthearted and joke with others at work, but when I get home, I seem to tense up and take things too seriously."

Don't be discouraged if laughter and fun don't exactly describe the atmosphere at your house. Some of us find it easy to joke and laugh; others of us have to work at it. If you need a little help, try these suggestions:

- *Spend some time looking through old scrapbooks and photo albums.* When our kids were growing up, we sometimes pulled out our college yearbooks and wedding pictures. The boys got lots of chuckles out of seeing their mom as a college majorette.

- *See a funny movie or read a funny book together.* Or you can cut out funny cartoons from the newspaper and put them in a prominent place, such as on the refrigerator or a bulletin board.

- *Play with your kids—games that they want to play.* Don't be ashamed to play something, even if you are inept. (You don't have to be a great basketball player to play a round of H-O-R-S-E.) This will make the game even funnier to your children. And it will be good for your humility!

- *Be vulnerable to your kids and learn to laugh at yourself.* Did you do something silly? Admit it! Did something funny happen to you today? Share it!

Tip #2
Let Surprises Add Spice To Your Family Life

Every home needs to operate with a certain level of routine. But that doesn't mean that family life has to be boring. Every once in a while, we need to break out of our routines and do something unexpected. Family relationships are refreshed and stimulated when an element of surprise is added from time to time.

I (Claudia) clearly remember the morning I decided to surprise my family and break out of our breakfast rut. As my crew gathered around the breakfast table and took their seats, they were confronted by a *huge* bowl of freshly popped popcorn. At each place setting was a small bowl, and on each face was confused amazement. The expression was easy to read: *this time Mom has really flipped.*

I explained that because popcorn is corn, and many breakfast cereals are made from corn, they should think of their unusual meal as having cereal for breakfast. I remember one son's parting comment: "Gee, Mom, we should have a strange breakfast at least once a month!"

If popcorn for breakfast doesn't thrill you, why not try a recipe for (almost) nutritious cookies made with whole-wheat flour, oatmeal, raisins, or peanut butter (or a combination)? While we wouldn't recommend cookies as a steady diet, they make an interesting breakfast occasionally—especially on a nonschool day. Want to be really crazy? Serve pancakes or waffles with ice cream instead of butter!

Here are some other ways you can surprise your family:

- "Kidnap" your spouse or your child and take him or her out for a special treat.

- Throw a party for a normally unheralded event, like the dog's birthday or the first snowfall.

Have "Blue Foods Night"

"Blue foods night" can be tricky, since there are few naturally blue foods. But if you can tolerate a night of less-than-optimum nutrition, tint several foods with blue food coloring and serve them together at dinnertime. Canned pears, mashed potatoes, rice, milk, pancakes, and waffles all take a tint fairly well. You can even throw in a science lesson by cutting the ends off celery sticks and soaking the cut ends in a strong solution of blue food coloring and water. Do this a couple of days ahead of time, and let your children observe the progress of the blue color up the veins of the celery to the leaves. Surprise them by serving the celery stuffed with blue-tinted cream cheese!

- Do something out of character—such as wearing a fake nose to the dinner table!
- Switch places at the dinner table and have everyone act like the person who usually sits in that place. (Be kind!)
- Declare tonight's dinnertime "Backward Night." Have everyone put their clothes on backward, turn their chairs around backward, and eat dessert first!

Tip #3
Find Alternatives to Television

When our children were young, the only electronic attention-grabber we had to worry about was the television. Now, of course, parents are competing for their children's time not only with the TV but also with computers and video games. Our intention here is not to debate the pros and cons of TV or computers and video games. We have our favorite TV programs, and computers are obviously handy for homework and research. But if all you or your children do is spend time in front of electronic screens, paying little or no attention to one another, your family connectedness is in big trouble.

Consider these creative alternatives:

- *Read together as a family.* Go to your local library and let your children choose a book they would enjoy. Then read and discuss it together.

- *Listen to a radio program together.* Afterward, discuss what you heard. Or buy some radio dramas on cassette or CD and listen to them together.

- *Visit an art gallery or museum.* Make it an outing for the whole family. Conclude the excursion with a snack or drink while you talk about what you saw, asking one another, "What did you like? What didn't you like?"

- *Attend a live drama.* It doesn't have to be a professional show; a high school or other amateur production can be just as entertaining. Check with local schools or civic associations for upcoming events.

- *Attend a concert.* Many local orchestras have free outdoor concerts. Or invest in tickets to the symphony—if you are willing to train your children in proper etiquette for such functions. Look for performances that are particularly geared to children, such as *Peter and the Wolf.*

- *Check out local sporting events.* Don't stop with your favorites—consider sports you may be less familiar with, such as hockey, track and field, tennis, or skating.

- *Have friends over for an evening.* Play board games, have a sing-along, hold a storytelling competition, or play charades. Your kids may yet discover the best entertainment isn't on an electronic screen!

Stick Together—Have a Taffy Pull

If you want to re-create an old-time family memory builder and have some old-fashioned family fun, try a taffy pull! You'll need to have at least one family member with a reasonably strong pair of arms or a teenager or two who want to work on building their biceps. A taffy pull is guaranteed to drain little ones of their energy. For brave and strong families, here's our recipe:

Taffy

Combine:
- *4 cups sugar*
- *2 cups karo*
- *2 cups cream*

Boil for 15 minutes. Add 1 envelope plain gelatin, dissolved in ½ cup water. Boil to 250 degrees. Pour in greased pans and let cool. As soon as cool enough to handle, pull taffy till white, then stretch out. Cut in pieces and wrap.[1]

Tip #4
Celebrate Your Family

How long has it been since you've had a celebration at your house? Too often we wait for special events to come along like birthdays and official holidays, and then we're rushed. No

Create a Backyard Circus

Are you looking for a great birthday party suggestion? Or maybe an idea for a party for no reason at all? Consider a backyard circus! Your children will enjoy being in on the planning and preparation.

The first step is to make an invitation list. With younger children a good rule is to arrange to have one helper (older child, teen, or other parent) for every five children. For fun invitations, use felt markers to write on inflated balloons. Let the air out and send one balloon to each guest. Ask each guest to dress as a favorite circus performer (clown, acrobat, animal trainer, and so on) and to bring a favorite "wild" stuffed animal.

Decorate large cardboard boxes as cages for transporting the "wild" animals. Almost anything can be used to decorate the boxes—finger paint, felt markers, tempera paints, leftover pieces of wallpaper, wrapping paper, or fabric. Attach strings to the fronts of the boxes and connect all the boxes with the string.

Mark off circus rings in the yard using rope, string, the garden hose, or anything else that can be shaped into a circle. Each ring then becomes a performance area for the costumed guests. Let each ring take turns performing for the others. One ring could feature singers; another, acrobats or dancers; another, jugglers; another, clowns. Play happy music to add to the atmosphere.

After the performances serve—what else?—animal crackers and juice. Then send your happy performers home with lots of fun memories.

wonder so many celebrations feel more like obligations! What can we do to change this and add some fun and excitement to our family life?

We don't have to wait for a big event—but we do have to slow down. In fact, why not stop right now and spend a few moments thinking about those special people around you? Think about the events and activities that will be going on in their lives over the next few weeks, and see if you can discover some reason for celebrating. For example:

- Celebrate significant milestones. Perhaps a teen got that treasured driver's license or a young child learned to dress him- or herself this week.

- Celebrate noteworthy accomplishments, such as a spouse's promotion, a music recital, or a sports victory.

- Celebrate anniversaries—say, the anniversary of the morning the stray cat came to join your family, or the anniversary of the day you moved into your present home.

- Celebrate the natural beauty of the sunset or the leaves changing color.

- Celebrate when something comes to an end—when the braces are removed or the final car payment is made.

- Celebrate for no reason at all!

Tip #5
Read Together as a Family

Have you ever taken a trip to Narnia? If not, let us tell you how to get your travel ticket: invest in your own set of books from The Chronicles of Narnia series by C. S. Lewis. Then get ready for a great trip! The ideal time to visit Narnia is when your children are elementary age. That's when we traveled there. In the evening after dinner and before bedtime, we would curl up in the living room and read aloud as the main characters, Edmund, Lucy, Susan, and Peter, traveled to Narnia and encountered Aslan the lion and many other memorable characters.

That Christmas, Aslan, a lovable stuffed lion, came to live with us. He kept Narnia alive for us long after the last book was completed. Many years later, Aslan—grubby but much loved—still lives in our den.

Why not invest in a trip to Narnia? You may start a family reading tradition! Some other good books to read as a family are *Pilgrim's Progress* (look for a children's edition); *Hans Brinker, or the Silver Skates*, *A Christmas Carol*, and *Alice in Wonderland*.

Overcoming the Blahs

Are the winter blahs getting you and your family down? January is a prime time for the blahs. The holiday excitement is over. The holiday bills are piling up. The weather can be depressing. It seems as if there's no more fun to be squeezed out of life.

If your family has been hit by the winter blahs, try some of these suggestions to chase away the doldrums:

- Try a new recipe. As you enjoy eating it, have each one at the table share something he or she would like to do next summer.

- Call or write someone you haven't contacted in a long time; write a note of encouragement to someone you know is having problems.

- Lay a checkered tablecloth on the living-room floor and have an indoor picnic.

- Window-shop with a twist: list all the things you see in the store windows or catalogs that you already have. Most of us have more than we realize. Then thank God for your abundance of blessings.

- Visit a nursing home or hospital. Many people in these institutions rarely get visitors, especially in January.

- Organize a neighborhood snowball fight or snowman-building contest.

Projects for Playing and Having Fun Together

Project #1
Make a Family Slide, Video, or PowerPoint Show

It was a cold, rainy, dreary weekend. Dave was away on business, and I (Claudia) was at home with three boys whose energy levels did not match the weather. The prospect of an entire weekend stuck in an apartment with three antsy children was not thrilling to a mom who was already tired from the hectic week that had just passed.

Out of desperation, our favorite family slide show was born. The boys and I decided to assemble a slide show as a surprise for Dad. Starting with pictures back in our pre-marriage days and continuing through the birth of each child, our slide show began to take shape. An accompanying audiotape captured the magical moments as each boy narrated his birth and early years. It turned out to be such a fun project that we hardly noticed the rain outside.

Many years and several grandchildren later, our grown sons and their families surprised me on a major-milestone birthday with a PowerPoint slide show, featuring sage bits of advice from the younger set on how to age gracefully, along with captivating digital photos of the world's most adorable grandchildren (ours, of course!). The technology had changed, but the principle—capturing happy memories—remained the same.

How you go about capturing the memories on durable media will depend upon your resources. You may want to use a slide projector and film (yes, they still make those things!), a video recorder, or the latest digital equipment, including scanners and creative computer software. Include memories from the past, either by scanning photos on the computer or by going low-tech and filming pages from your photo albums with a video camera. Whatever equipment you use, have the children write a funny script. It can be recorded to play along with the photos, or it can be acted out (which is what our sons did for my birthday presentation).

Later, plan a special family time for the premiere. If possible, let the children work the equipment. Creating, producing, and directing their own family show will give them a great sense of accomplishment.

A postscript: if you make a show with a video camera because that's all you have, find someone who can burn the presentation onto a CD for you. Always try to upgrade your presentations to keep up with the latest technology. Ask someone born in the 1950s what they wouldn't give for the ability to watch their parents' old 16-millimeter, black-and-white home movies again, or to be able to listen to their own baby talk and childish prattle recorded on those old reel-to-reel tapes!

Project #2
Have a Treasure-Hunt Dinner

Everyone loves to think about hidden treasure, and most of us have dreamed about finding one—at least, we did when we were kids! Here's a memory builder that will translate a treasure-hunting fantasy into reality for your children: a treasure-hunt dinner. Plan a simple meal with lots of finger foods that are easy to hide, such as carrots, bananas, dinner rolls, and celery sticks. Cover the foods in plastic wrap and hide them in various places throughout your home—in drawers and closets, under the furniture, and so on. Divide the meal into courses and give your children a handwritten clue about where to find the first part of their meal. After each course give them another clue to lead them to the next part of the meal. If you want to be clever, write each clue in a rhyming couplet.

Have your hunters eat each course as they discover it. After the hot main course (keep it simple—hot dogs are good), give a clue that directs your children to get their baths and put on their pajamas. Then give them a clue for dessert, such as a hidden cookie. When the treasure-hunt dinner is finished, the children are ready for bed, and Mom and Dad can have a treasured meal alone, complete with candlelight, music, and conversation! Or, if you're a single parent, treat yourself to your own favorite meal and curl up with a good book or arrange for a baby-sitter beforehand and go out for the evening with a friend.

If you're ambitious, you can adapt this idea as a theme for a birthday party and include a homemade "treasure chest" with small prizes for each child at the end of the search. You can customize the idea for your little pirates, knights, or space explorers, using whatever props your imagination and their willing hands can come up with.

Project #3
Plan for Sanity in the Summertime

Too many parents just let the summer happen—with insane results. But the end of the school year doesn't have to mean that all sanity in your home goes out the window. It's possible to have sanity in the summertime if you're willing to put forth a little effort. The key word is *planning*. Start weeks or even months before summer by asking yourself these three questions:

- *"What?"* What do you want to see happen this summer? For instance, do you want to develop a closer relationship with your children? Do you want to work on communication or building your children's self-esteem? Set goals for the summer based on your answers to the "what?" question. Remember to include a personal goal for yourself and a goal for your marriage, such as having a weekly date night or taking a twenty-four-hour getaway.

- *"How?"* This question is very practical. What can you do to reach your goals? List possible activities. For instance, to work on communication, maybe you'll make finger puppets and use open-ended questions to help your child open up and talk.

- *"When?"* Make a tentative schedule for the summer. For instance, maybe every Wednesday can be children's day, when you set aside time to do special things with your children. Maybe Mom and Dad can get a baby-sitter each Saturday afternoon.

Project #4
Make Your Own Family Roots Book

These days many people, with the aid of the Internet and other resources, are compiling their family genealogies—their "roots." While that's a fine hobby, you can do something far simpler—and maybe even more fun!—with your children: create your own "family roots book."

A fancy journal, a scrapbook, or even a plain notebook will do. Assemble an assortment of pens, pencils, stickers, scrap paper, and creative minds. Ask each family member to write down all the clever, ridiculous, happy, and disastrous things they can remember about themselves on the pieces of scrap paper. Then ask them to do the same for the other family members (being kind, of course). Compile the best selections in your family roots book, adding appropriate artwork or stickers. Record whatever your hearts desire—funny sayings, family happenings, interesting news about friends and relatives.

One woman we know kept up a family roots book for sixteen years. She said it never failed to entertain her family as they read about:

- Kelly, who at four sincerely thought she could fly and designed elaborate costumes for her attempts

- Stewart, who fell sound asleep on top of all the family baggage at a New York City airport

- Susie, who logically announced, "I can tie my shoes, bounce the basketball under my knees, and even blow my nose. I must be six instead of four."

Think you're getting a late start? That's OK. Start your family roots book now. It's never too late to begin cataloging memories!

The smartest advice on raising children is to enjoy them while they are still on your side.

—UNKNOWN

CONCLUSION

Now It's Your Turn: Taking the Next Step

Through these pages, we have looked together at seven key connections that can help create strong and healthy families. We hope that what you've read has been encouraging to you. Perhaps you have strong connections in one or several of these areas, and you've seen your own family within these pages. It's always good to know we are doing some things right!

Maybe you've also noted some areas that need a little attention in your family. We hope you will take our tips seriously. We also hope you'll work on developing stronger family connections by utilizing some of the easy, fun, and practical projects we've recommended.

Wherever you are, however connected or disconnected you consider your family to be, let us remind you: all families are in process. There are no perfect families. Our family definitely wasn't perfect. We made our share of parenting mistakes—just ask our kids! But if you ask them if we love them, they will say yes. If you ask them if they love us, they will say yes. And if you ask them if we are all committed to one another, they will say yes once again.

Did we teach our children how to have perfect families? Absolutely not. As we observe our sons and their families, we have to admit that their families aren't perfect either. (Of course, our eight grandchildren come close to perfection!)

What we are trying to say is that we never *arrive* as families. But we can continue to love and support each other along the way.

One day, like us, you will be able to enjoy the fruits of your labor. You will be able to have wonderful relationships with your adult children and grandchildren. But you have to start now. You have to love your family now and work on building those connections. Whether your children are toddlers or teens, it's not too late!

You may be thinking, *Won't developing strong family connections take a lot of time and work?* Yes, but we promise you, it will be worth it—and not just afterward, but throughout the process. Let us encourage you: don't short-cut or wish away the parenting years! We know four families who tried to. They concocted a joint vacation plan one summer in which they rented a vacation house together for two months. Each couple took turns spending two weeks at the vacation house taking care of all thirteen of their collective children.

"You've got to be kidding!" someone commented to one of the dads. "I wouldn't call taking care of thirteen children a vacation!"

"Oh, the two weeks were a horrendous disaster," the dad admitted. "The vacation was the six weeks at home without the kids!"

We may laugh, but how many parents wish their children would grow up and leave home? How many have separated themselves psychologically from their children? How many have allowed a negative attitude to influence their parental outlook? How many would say they have more fun without their children than with them? *Enjoy parenting my children?* they think. *Who are you kidding?*

The truth is, when we rush through life, wishing for the next stage to hurry up and get here, relationships tend to suffer. Communication breaks down, and confusion reigns. Too many parents hurry through the parenting years and then, on the other end, find they missed out on building a strong, connected family—and on having fun together in the process. Take it from two who know how fast the years go by: *now* is the time to enjoy your children and parenting. One mother summed up the urgency of enjoying your family now in this little meditation called "Wet Oatmeal Kisses":

> The baby is teething. The children are fighting. Your husband just called and said, "Eat dinner without me." One of these days you'll explode and shout to the kids,

"Why don't you grow up and act your age?" And they will.

Or, "You guys get outside and find yourselves something to do. And don't slam that door!" And they don't.

You'll straighten their bedrooms all neat and tidy, toys displayed on the shelf, hangers in the closet, animals caged. You'll yell, "Now I want it to stay this way!" And it will.

You'll say, "I want complete privacy on the phone. No screaming. Do you hear me?" And no one will answer.

No more plastic tablecloths stained with pasta sauce. No more dandelion bouquets. No more iron-on patches. No more knotted shoelaces, muddy boots, or rubber bands for ponytails.

Imagine—a lipstick with a point, no baby-sitter for New Year's Eve, washing clothes only once a week. No silly school plays where your child is a tree. No blaring stereos.

No more Christmas presents made of paste and toothpicks. No wet oatmeal kisses. No more tooth fairy. No more giggles in the dark, scraped knees to kiss, or sticky fingers to clean. Only a voice asking, "Why don't you grow up?" And the silence echoes, "I did."[1]

Trust us: all the hard, crazy, wonderful, frustrating years of parenting are worth it. If you put in the time and effort now, in the future you will experience the joy of seeing your children reach adulthood. You will have the satisfaction of seeing them well launched into the world. And your relationships with your adult children—not to mention any grandchildren they produce—will be their own reward.

Now is the time to invest in your family, to push the positives, to have great talks. To deal with disagreements with grace. To teach your children responsibility and how to worship together, pray together, and play together. Now is the time not only to discover the key connections of strong, healthy families, but to take the next step and make those connections a reality in your home.

Projects for Taking the Next Step

Project #1
Adopt a Family Motto

While we have included this project in our conclusion, it may be one you'll want to start with! The Bible tells us, "As [a man] thinks in his heart, so is he" (Proverbs 23:7 NKJV). What thoughts have you been thinking about your family? Are they positive or negative? Do you realize your thoughts are shaping your family, whether or not you intend to do so?

If you've been thinking negative thoughts, you can counter them by adopting a positive family motto. Your family motto can be displayed in a prominent place, so everyone in the family can be reminded of it on a regular basis. Get together as a family, make a list of possible mottos, then choose one. It may be something like, "In our family we build each other up. Others will tear us down." Or, "In our family we attack problems, not each other."

You can have more than one family motto. We've had several over the years. Some have even been silly or humorous, such as, "No problem is too big that a bowl of ice cream won't solve it," and, "Every family needs a little insanity to keep its sanity!"

Project #2
Set Family Goals

We want to close this book by challenging you to set some goals that will help you strengthen your family connections. Of course, setting goals is one thing; accomplishing them is another. So follow through! Here are a few goals you can start with:

- Find some way each day to let your family members know you love them.

- Don't let any member of your family feel left out or not cared for.

- Remember that each member of your family is an individual. Let them be who they are and appreciate them for who they are. Don't try to make them over into the people you wish they were. You don't want to produce clones!

- Do everything you can to make your home a fun place to be.

- Try to say things to members of your family that lift them up, not drag them down.

- Don't fret about the past or worry about the future. Live each day to the fullest as it comes along. We can't do anything about yesterday, and tomorrow is unsure. Today is the day!

Notes

Introduction: Before You Begin

1. Dolores Curran, *Traits of a Heathy Family* (Minneapolis: Winston Press, 1983).

2. Manny Feldman, "A Family Is," quoted in our book, *Sixty One-Minute Family-Builders* (Brentwood, Tenn.: Wolgemuth & Hyatt: 1989), 115–16. Also found on the Web site "Poems and Thoughts for Genealogists" at http://www.g8dhe.com/edna/poems_and_thoughts_for_genealog.htm.

Connection One: Spending Time Together

1. Pat King, *How to Have All the Time You Need Every Day* (Carol Stream, Ill.: Tyndale, 1980).

2. Ross Campbell, *How to Really Love Your Child* (Wheaton, Ill.: Victor, 1981).

3. Adapted from http://www.ianr.unl.edu/pubs/family/nf439.htm.

Connection Two: Pushing the Positives

1. B. Achord, M. Berry, G. Harding, K. Kerber, S. Scott, and L. O. Schwab, *Building Family Strengths: A Manual for Families* (Lincoln, Neb.: University of Nebraska-Lincoln,

Departments of Human Development and Family and Conferences and Institutes, March 1986), 42.

Connection Three: Talking to Each Other—and Really Listening

1. Adapted from Alan Loy McGinnis's book, *The Friendship Factor* (Minneapolis: Augsburg, 1979).

Connection Four: Handling Stress and Disagreements with Grace

1. Fritz Ridenour, *What Teenagers Wish Their Parents Knew About Kids* (Waco, Tex.: Word, 1982), 172.

2. Adapted from *The Strong-Willed Child* by James Dobson (Carol Stream, Ill.: Tyndale, 1977). For more tips on how to avoid guilt and anxiety as you parent your spirited child, please refer to our book, *Answering the 8 Cries of the Spirited Child* (West Monroe, La.: Howard, 2003).

Connection Five: Working Together and Promoting Responsibility

1. Dorothy Law Nolte, "Children Learn What They Live." Copyright 1972/1975 by Dorothy Law Nolte. A free poster of this poem is provided at the Web site www.EmpowermentResources.com.

Connection Six: Promoting Spiritual Well-Being

1. Achord, et al., *Building Family Strengths.*

Connection Seven: Playing and Having Fun Together

1. From the *Amish Country Cookbook*, Volume 1 (Nappanee, Ind.: Evangel Publishing House, 1979), 192. Used by permission.

Conclusion: Now It's Your Turn: Taking the Next Step

1. Author unknown. From Ann Landers's syndicated column, *The Knoxville Journal*, February 21, 1986, A-8.

Other Resources from David and Claudia Arp Include:

Books

Answering the 8 Cries of the Spirited Child
No Time for Sex
10 Great Dates to Energize Your Marriage
10 Great Dates Before You Say "I Do"
10 Great Dates for Empty Nesters
Loving Your Relatives
The Second Half of Marriage
Fighting for Your Empty Nest Marriage
New Baby Stress
Suddenly They're 13!
Quiet Whispers from God's Heart for Couples
52 Fantastic Dates for You and Your Mate
The Big Book of Family Fun

Video Curricula

10 Great Dates to Energize Your Marriage
The Second Half of Marriage
PEP Groups for Moms
PEP Groups for Parents of Teens

About Marriage Alive International, Inc.

Marriage Alive International, Inc., founded by husband-wife team Claudia Arp and David Arp, MSW, is a nonprofit marriage and family enrichment ministry dedicated to providing resources, seminars, and training to empower churches to help build better marriages and families. Marriage Alive also works with community organizations, the U.S. military, schools, and businesses.

The Arps are marriage and family educators and have been involved in marriage and family ministry in the USA and in Europe for more than twenty-five years. David and Claudia authored an Occasional Paper for the United Nations' International Year of the Family and spent several months at the United Nations in Vienna, Austria, researching how family traditions are passed down through the generations. Marriage Alive seminars are popular across the United States and in Europe.

The mission of Marriage Alive is to train and empower leaders who invest in others by building strong marriage and family relationships through the integration of biblical truth, contemporary research, practical application, and fun.

Marriage Alive Resources and Services include:

- Marriage and family books in eight languages
- Video-based educational programs
- Marriage and parenting seminars
- Consulting, training, leadership development, coaching and mentoring

Contact Marriage Alive at www.marriagealive.com

CONNECTING

Use these pages to record some of the successes you've had connecting with your family.

CONNECTION ONE: Spending Time Together

_____
_____
_____
_____
_____
_____
_____

Connection Two: Pushing the Positives

_____

_____

_____

_____

_____

Connection Three: Talking to Each Other—and Really Listening

_____

_____

_____

_____

_____

Connection Four: Handling Stress and Disagreements with Grace

_____

_____

_____

_____

_____

CoNNECTIoN Five: Working Together and Promoting Responsibility

_____

_____

_____

_____

_____

CoNNECTIoN Six: Promoting Spiritual Well-Being

_____

_____

_____

_____

_____

CoNNECTIoN Seven: Playing and Having Fun Together

_____

_____

_____

_____

_____

_____

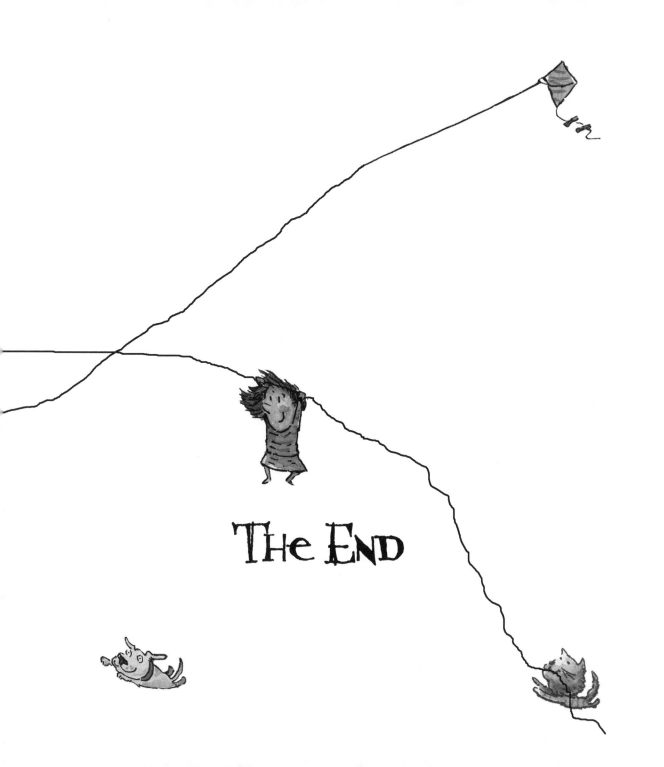

The End

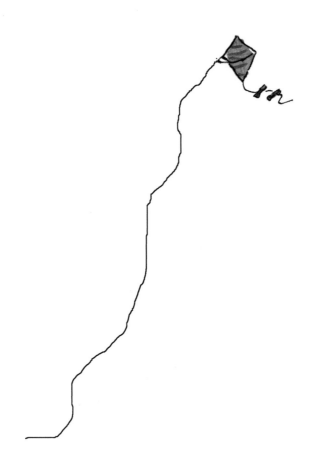